The System Approach

PUBLICATIONS

Hanser Gardner Publications
Cincinnati, OH

The System Approach

A Strategy to Survive and Succeed In the Global Economy

By

Dr. K. (Subbu) Subramanian

Library of Congress Cataloging-in-Publication Data

Subramanian, K. (Krishnamoorthy), 1949-
   The system approach : a strategy to survive and succeed in the global economy / by K. (Subbu) Subramanian.
      p. cm.
   Includes bibliographical references and index.
   ISBN 1-56990-255-0
   1. Capitalism. 2. Competition, International. 3. Structural adjustment (Economic policy) 4. Globalization. I. Title.

HB501 .S9319 2000
658'.045--dc21

00-034740

While the advice and information in The System Approach are believed to be true, accurate, and reliable, neither the author nor the publisher can accept any legal responsibility for any errors, omissions, or damages that may arise out of the use of this advice and information. The author and publisher make no warranty of any kind, expressed or implied, with regard to the material contained in this work.

The opinions expressed in this book are solely those of the author. They do not represent the opinions of Norton Co. or Saint Gobain Abrasives. All characters mentioned in this book are fictitious. They do not refer to any person or individuals in real life.

A **MODERN MACHINE SHOP** book
published by
Gardner Publications, Metalworking's Premier Publisher
www.mmsonline.com

Hanser Gardner Publications
6915 Valley Avenue
Cincinnati, OH 45244-3029
www.hansergardner.com

Copyright © 2000 by Hanser Gardner Publications. All rights reserved. No part of this book, or parts thereof, may be reproduced, stored in a retrieval system, or transmitted in any form or by any means without the express written consent of the publisher.

2 3 4 5 6   05

Table of Contents

Chapter 1. The Impact of Global Capitalism 1

Chapter 2. Global Economy—Separating the Myths from Reality 27

Chapter 3. The System Approach 51

Chapter 4. The Enterprise and the System Approach 71

Chapter 5. The System Approach for Industrial Processes 95

Chapter 6. The System Approach as a Strategic Tool in the Global Economy 121

Chapter 7. Personal Concerns and the Systems Approach 149

Chapter 8. A Glimmer of Hope 193

Appendix 209

References 215

To:
All my teachers
and my advisor: Professor Nathan H. Cook

PREFACE

"Global Economy" is now a familiar term to almost everyone. Yet, it means something different for each person, depending on the individual: young or old, blue collar or white collar, professional working in the manufacturing sector or service sector, working for a large company, or small company, and so on.

The Global Economy has meant many different things to this author over a professional career spanning more than two decades. Early on, working for a large automotive company with strictly assigned tasks and organizations, the Global Economy implied a large cloud hanging over the corporation. But this giant cloud did not seem to inhibit or affect anyone in the day-to-day operations until a decade or so later. In the meantime, the opportunities and resources seemed limitless for the few who showed initiative to "solve the problem" while maintaining due respect for the assigned tasks and organizational boundaries. A few years later, the phrase Global Economy took on a meaning that was very serious and ominous. This was the time when large U.S. corporations—many which had existed for a century or more—slowly caved in. They were restructured, downsized, and in some cases sent to oblivion. In the last decade of the 20th century, the Global Economy came to represent a more vibrant and dynamic set of possibilities, constantly in resonance with an impending crisis—a wave that one can surf with joy even while in danger of being swept off balance without notice.

Along with these larger views of the Global Economy, there has been an underlying personal need for a large number of professionals employed in manufacturing and in other industries through out the world: the need to survive and succeed. This book is a summary of a methodology—the System Approach—that would seem to evolve from such experiences, both personal and from observations of the success and failure of countless fellow professionals.

This book opens with a fictional episode that highlights the issues faced by an industrial worker in the Global Economy, followed by a series of references pertaining to real life experiences that were extracted from recent books and magazines. But "Global Economy" is not the evil scheme of a few. Instead, it is a natural evolution of issues and opportunities arising out of developments in certain technology areas. This viewpoint leads to the conclusion that one need not accept the Global Economy as an inevitable dark cloud. Instead, it can be viewed as an opportunity to harness resources from anywhere in the world. It can also be viewed as an opportunity to deliver results that impact all potential users worldwide. This type of strategic thinking can be pursued by any individual employee and by his/her organization or company. Such approaches to success in the Global Economy can be synergistic between the individual employee and his/her employer. And a strategic approach can be initiated and implemented by an individual employee at any level in an enterprise, thanks to the Global Economy which provides the potential for employers to cultivate and foster global strategies to harness worldwide opportunities.

In Chapter 3, the methodology for the systematic and organized pursuit of opportunities in the Global Economy, called the "System Approach," is introduced. This approach calls for a fundamental shift in our thinking—a transition from performing task-oriented job assignments to participation in a system-oriented problem solving process. The chapters that follow are intended to further elucidate this methodology and explain how it can be used in industrial activities at any level—from the management of the enterprise as a whole, to achieving quantum improvements in industrial processes, or in the systematic career development of individual employees.

The concluding chapters highlight the use of the System Approach. In Chapter 7, the job functions of various employees—an enterprise manager, professional engineers, supervisors, product managers, production workers, and a college professor—are examined to illustrate how each of these job functions can benefit from the System Approach. The final chapter returns to our earlier fictional episode (Chapter 1) and illustrates how the System Approach has the potential to change and positively impact the life of every employee in our industrial society.

We are primarily a nation of immigrants. Hence, our willingness to change and adapt is limitless. The traditional, historic and cultural barriers that govern and slow the rate of change of many older nations are not barriers to our nation's march for change and progress. At the same time, we as a nation count on individual responsibility to recognize and accommodate change. This book has been written as a modest effort to provide a means or methodology for fellow professionals, as well as for industrial organizations, to recognize the need for change in the Global Economy and how to cope with such changes, with a vision towards long-term success. This methodology is called the System Approach, a *Strategy to Survive and Succeed in the Global Economy*.

K. (Subbu) Subramanian.

ACKNOWLEDGMENTS

The methodology and guidelines summarized in this book are a product of evolutionary experiences. Hence, this book is truly a cumulative outcome with inputs from a large number of people with whom I have had the good fortune to work with as colleagues, customers, fellow professionals, peers, reports and supervisors. This list of people to whom I owe gratitude is rather large. My sincere and personal thanks to all of them.

My opportunity to experience a diversity of situations in the Global Economy occurred thanks to my professional career at Norton Co. (now part of Saint Gobain Abrasives), and earlier at Ford Motor Co. and the International Harvester Co. Every day of this professional journey has been and continues to be a learning experience. My sincere thanks to all those involved in the management of these companies for the opportunities and the experiences I have derived from them.

At the risk of inadvertently leaving out a few, I would like to express my special thanks to some people for their specific contributions to this project.

The seed or idea for this book was planted by Mr. Chris Koepfer, Senior Editor, *Modern Machine Shop*. Mr. Woody Chapman, Editorial Director, Hanser Gardner Publications concurred with the idea. Woody also displayed extraordinary patience and offered continued encouragement and guidance throughout the writing and formation of this book. Without them, there would have been no book.

There are many who offered their input, guidance and encouragement at various stages during the preparation of this manuscript. To mention a few: Dr. Bruce Kramer, NSF; Dr. Jay Lee, NSF; Prof. Alex Slocum, MIT; Prof. Mohamad Noori, WPI; Dr. S. Ramaswamy, MKPA; Dr. N. Balasubramanian, Bristol-Myers Squibb; Prof. John Wilkes, WPI; Prof. Kash Rangan, Harvard Business School; Prof. Marco Iansiti, Harvard Business School; Mr. E. L. Lambert, HGTC; Dr. Wei Jing Chia, Saint Gobain Abrasives, and Ms. Mary E.

Porter, Saint Gobain Abrasives. I acknowledge each of them with thanks for their contributions.

Special thanks to all my colleagues at the worldwide locations of Saint Gobain Abrasives and at the Higgins Grinding Technology Center. The successes derived through their efforts with their customers—both internal and external—are the real life testimonials for the benefits of the System Approach described in this book.

I would also like to thank the faculty members and students at various universities with whom I have had extensive dialogue and discussions on this subject. Thanks also to my fellow professionals in the SME and the ASME. Members of these and other professional societies truly represent the core of the engineering resources for the manufacturing industries. This book in many respects stems from their needs and aspirations, and to finding a methodology to satisfy them.

My gratitude to Ms. Janice Vasalofsky is endless. Her help, patience and assistance in the preparation of this manuscript and the revisions are truly appreciated. Her energy and enthusiasm helped a great deal to push forward to the finish line, after two years of effort.

I offer special thanks to my wife Durga and our son Ganesh. I fully appreciate their patience and forbearance for all my time away from family life, while I was engaged in writing. Further, I appreciate the challenges from my wife—also a fellow professional—on many viewpoints expressed in this book, which helped me to refine my concepts and logic.

Finally, my thanks to you, the reader. I hope you have as much fun reading this book as I had writing it!

Chapter 1
The Impact of Global Capitalism

A Bad Dream

Paul Gagnon was seated in a comfortable chair in the conference room. His Supervisor, Mary Patterson, a young and successful engineer in the company sat immediately to his right. It was a new and strange experience for Paul. As a production worker in the company, he had never before attended a meeting with so many managers, not to mention a politician. In the room with Paul and Mary were Joe Whitehead—the Design Manager, Linda Cook—the Financial Controller, Ralph McCarthy—the district's Congressman, and Jack Singer—President of the Operating Unit.

"Shall we get started," signaled Jack, trying to get everyone's attention. "As you all know, we have always relied heavily on worker productivity to keep us ahead of our competition, and it is now at an all time high. I have never seen our work force work as hard, or perform any better than they are doing at the present time. We have installed the best information systems which, by the way, has helped to wring out significant cost reductions in our operation in the past two years."

Paul shifted slowly in his chair, feeling some discomfort about what he had just heard. By "significant cost reduction," Mr. Singer was referring to the layoff of about 40 people from the company, a 25% workforce reduction. "Hadn't the Human Resources Manager, Scott Healey, described the layoff as "reengineering?" reflected Paul.

"Our profitability, even though it is not as high as I would like it to be, is not bad." Jack was speaking again. "Yet, there is a lot of uneasiness, on all levels. On the one hand, we want our workers to be committed and loyal, yet I do not know of any way of assuring them of our commitment to their employment. As you know, these are not the good old days, when we could reasonably say that a person was hired for a lifetime, as long as he or she did a good job. Doing the very best in a given job does not seem to be good enough any more. Yesterday, at the corporate meeting, I heard talk of acquisitions and mergers. The guys at the top feel that we cannot be competitive, even with all our improvements. One option being talked about is moving the entire operation to an offshore location. I simply don't get it," continued Jack with a sense of frustration that was clearly shared by everyone in the room. "Well, why don't we go around the room and see what's on everyone's mind? As you know, we called this meeting to get everyone's points of view on our current situation and where we are headed."

"This is not the Jack Singer I've heard so much about," thought Paul Gagnon. "Whatever happened to the orderly introductions and the carefully stated outline of objectives for the meeting? Jack is renowned for his procedure and organization—clearly, something is definitely wrong. Maybe he senses something serious, but can't get a grip on the problem."

Joe Whitehead, the Design Manager, spoke next. "In the past five years, my department has shrunk by 50%. I have lost most of my key design talent—the draftsman, the engineer in charge of heat transfer analysis, the design details engineer—each one of them has been let go through our reengineering effort. We now do most of our design analysis overseas and download them through the Internet. The way things are going, we may not even need many design options if our customers buy their subassemblies from our competition instead of buying our components and assembling them, as they do now. The rumor is that our competitors plan to integrate the function of our components into their subassembly. This may even eliminate the need for our components altogether."

It occurred to Paul that Joe had always been politically correct.

"The days are getting longer and harder." Mary Patterson, the Manufacturing Engineer, had jumped into the discussion. "When I came to this job three years ago, we had a tooling engineer, a quality engineer in charge of inspection, and a maintenance technician, and my responsibility was process development. Today, I seem to be everywhere. I don't mind that as long as I can see the light at the end of the tunnel. When I hear of acquisitions, mergers, and moves to offshore production, that concerns me a lot." Mary sighed as she slowly shook her head.

Linda Cook spoke next, offering her perspective as Financial Controller. "We have made capital investments at an unprecedented rate during the past few years. Yes, it's paying off, but not as much as it was supposed to. When I walk around the company, I get the sense that everyone looks at me as if I am the one to be blamed for all the layoffs. If everyone understood the basic economics, they would know for themselves what is happening and why," she lamented, while staring at the piles of accounting documents that were neatly arranged in binders in front of her.

"I simply don't understand it," said Congressman Ralph McCarthy in his slow drawl. "When I go to Washington, they tell me about all these wonderful numbers. The unemployment is low. The labor productivity is high. The U.S. economy is on the top. Yet, when I come home, all I hear is uneasiness and a sense of helplessness. Why isn't life the way it used to be—where everyone did their job and everyone knew what they were supposed to do? Is it because we have moved from a manufacturing economy to an information economy?"

Paul Gagnon looked around. Everyone else had offered opening remarks. It was now his turn to say something, but the only thoughts that came to his mind were about the uncertain future of his young son, David. "What will his life be like when he grows up? Will he be doing what I do, running a computer-controlled machine with built-in inspection tools? I have been busy studying and taking courses just to stay on top of my job. Several of my coworkers have been laid off, simply because they couldn't keep up with the technology. I have dreamed that David would one day be an engineer like Mary. But, after listening to Mary and Joe, I'm not sure anymore." Everyone in the room, the very people Paul had counted as role models for his son, appeared to be gloomy and dispirited.

Finally, Paul spoke. "I just don't know what to say. I really don't." He wondered if the others could detect the despair in his voice.

● ● ●

"Honey, it's time to wake up." Paul's wife Susan gave him a gentle shake. "You must have been having a nightmare. What is it you don't know? You said it over and over last night. 'I just don't know.' What does it mean?"

"It was all a bad dream, dear. I am glad it's over," Paul replied, as he woke up, pushed aside the sheets, and rose up from the bed.

"Honey, there is not enough time left for dreaming anymore," said Susan. "With three of our kids going to different schools and both of us working, I don't have a moment to rest, much less get a good night's sleep. I don't know how you manage to find time for all your dreams."

The Reality

It would be wonderful indeed if Paul Gagnon's dream had been just that—a dream. However, it is an inescapable reality that every one of us has experienced at least some of the concerns reflected in this fictional episode. The thoughts of Jack, Joe, Mary, Linda, Ralph, and Paul described in the dream are shades of real life experiences faced by millions of Americans in one way or another. Let's have a look at some of the evidence:

Example 1:

The cover story titled, "Economic Anxiety", in a recent issue of *BusinessWeek*[1] has the following subheading:

> *Ten years of downsizing and widening income inequality have taken an enormous social toll. U.S. workers are losing faith in their ability to prosper.*

The article goes on to describe the situation, as follows:

> *It starts with a rumor: A General Electric Company plant in the American Midwest is about to close its doors and move its operations to Mexico. A friend calls: Her brother turned down AT&T's buyout offer, only to be faced with immediate dismissal. You consider your future: A career change might be nice, but not an involuntary one. So, you rein in spending and ramp up savings, just to be safe.*
>
> *For millions of Americans, daily living has turned into a high-wire act for everyone—from the blue-collar worker who's eking out $5 an hour plucking chickens, to the bank teller whose job is being cut in a merger, to the midlevel executive who's now working out of his home as a consultant. It is a story that can't be told by the numbers,*

6 • The System Approach

because the numbers at times are misleading: 8 million jobs created in four years, the unemployment rate at 5.8%, inflation down to 2.7%, corporate profits on a four-year roll, and four years of economic recovery under our belts. "All the economic indicators are up...except mine," says Paul J. Szilagyi, 50, an unemployed North Miami Beach resident with a Ph.D. in chemistry.
(Additional excerpts from this reference are included in Appendix I.)

Example 2:

The following is an extract from a "Viewpoints" article from *Manufacturing Engineering* magazine.[2]

- *Knowledge Workers Sought:*

"Manufacturing concern seeks experts in all aspects of production and extended services for full time or temporary positions. Must be a self directed, innovative team player and willing to retrain on own time. Must be available evenings and weekends. Resumes by e-mail only to http://www.nextgenerationmanufacturing.com."

Long hours with an uncertain future, an employer who demands experience, but makes no commitment to invest in your future. Would you apply for such a job? Isn't this too far fetched? Maybe not.

Example 3:

The following is an extract from "Straight Talk," an article that appeared in *Industry Week* magazine.[3]

Ultrapreneurs get twice the work done in one work-hour as other executives—and their work is better and more productive. Who are these ultrapreneurs? How do they succeed and thrive in a global competitive world?

Example 4:

The following is an extract from the Vice President's Discussion, Council of Engineering Report of the ASME, 1997.[4]

> *The separation of the engineering disciplines, (e.g.) mechanical, electrical, chemical, is already falling away and in 25 years will be obsolete. As time moves forward, engineers need to do things that formerly were done by a whole team of engineers. The implications are that the engineers will need a broader and deeper education than they have had in the past. Engineering will become increasingly global no longer requiring that engineering be done in one place. The U.S. will not have a monopoly on engineering talent or capability.*

Example 5:

The following is an extract from the article, "Are Economists Obsolete Today?—New Economy, Old Thinking Threaten Profession," that appeared in *Investor's Business Daily*.[5]

> At first, old industrial giants, such as Inland Steel Industries Incorporated, fazed economists out. Now even data drenched firms are jettisoning them. "We didn't feel we needed to have economists on the staff. We eliminated the economics division of both companies," Wells Fargo spokeswoman Lorna Doubet said. When the San Francisco based firm needs economic analysis, it contracts out for it. "It is not that the information isn't needed any more. It is just that the economists are not providing it in the conventional way."
>
> But the new economy is neither static nor predictable. It is constantly changing, much like the rain forest. Yet, many economists still think they are observing a closed, controlled system.

Example 6:

The following is extracted from a book review article titled, "Is capitalism headed for a new Dark Age?"[6]

Japan's economy is stagnant, European unemployment is stuck in double digits and in the U.S., a presidential candidate is riding high by railing against a couple of pillars of the system: Free trade and the unfettered pursuit of corporate profits. Simultaneously, a vigorous and brutal global capitalism has emerged, one that promises prosperity to the multitudes while forcing enfeebled governments to kowtow to its commands.

*In **The Future of Capitalism**, Professor Lester Thurow concedes that no other system provides such gobs of efficiency and technology. But with no guiding ideology other than avarice, these very strengths could become the system's undoing. It operates in and often contributes to a world of growing economic imbalances. Missing is a set of common goals and values that citizens could rally behind. The upshot: Thurow warns that we could be slowly sinking into a new Dark Age.*

An overstatement? Let's hope so. But as Thurow takes us on this cheerless stroll past the perils confronting capitalism, he makes a convincing case that the marketplace lacks the magic to save the world from deep trouble. Other observers have covered much of this terrain: The challenges of sustaining a nation and maintaining wage levels in a global economy, worries about more frequent, ever deeper recessions, and the growth of intolerance and separatism. Thurow, to his credit, brings these problems into very sharp focus.

Example 7:

The following is an abstract from the article, "For workers, it's the age of anxiety," from the business section of the *Boston Globe*.[7] This article is based on a report from Massachusetts Incorporated, a think tank created by Mitchell Kertzman, Chief Executive Officer of Power Soft, a software company.

"The State of the American Dream in New England," an

in-depth look at economic life here, paints a sobering picture. People are working more hours to maintain their standard of living, often at the expense of family life and community involvement. Many have yet to recover the ground they lost during the last recession. They do work in a job market that is constantly demanding new skills and is often unforgiving of those who don't acquire them.

The well educated may feel stressed, but they are coping. They may even be thriving. For those without the benefit of a college education, the news is far less encouraging. Wages are falling, opportunities are disappearing, and the chances of landing a job with such basic middle-class staples as health insurance and pensions are diminishing.

"The broad middle-class is dividing into two distinct groups with very different profiles and prospects for long-term economic success," the study's authors write.

Example 8:

The following is an extract from the article, "What Price Good Jobs?" from the business section of the *Boston Globe*.[8]

> From 1988 to 1994, 10 out of 15 leading industrial states lost manufacturing jobs. In New England, all six states saw double-digit losses. This decline in manufacturing employment has forced state governments to offer tax credits to retain or attract the employers to their states. But no one seems to know how to break this costly cycle that critics say diverts scarce public dollars from other needs.

Example 9:

The following is an extract from the article, "How to Beat the Squeeze on the Middle Class", by Joseph S. Coyle (*Money Magazine*).[9]

> Say good-bye to security in all its forms: Job, pension, health care and financial. The web of comforts that mus-

cular U.S. companies and a benevolent Uncle Sam provided the American middle-class for 60 years is dissolving before your eyes. What's more, the burden of self-sufficiency heralded by today's it's-up-to-you mind-set will fall most broadly, if not always most painfully, on you—assuming you and yours are among the 52 million American households whose $25,000 to $100,000 incomes put them in what Money defines as the middle class.
(Additional excerpts from this reference are included in Appendix I.)

Example 10:
Finally, here is an excerpt from letter to the editor from a reader to the *Mechanical Engineering* magazine of the American Society of Mechanical Engineers.[10]

> To the Editor: In my position I have been greatly affected by these pseudo-engineers and am frustrated by the additional efforts I need to put forth to make up for their shortcomings. These shortcomings are almost invariably ignored by management in the name of lowering costs or increasing company profits at the expense of product quality and the morale of the degreed engineers. Why should I have to routinely sweep up after these people when I am paid only marginally more than them?

The Big Picture

The evidence presented above comes from a random selection of news clips found in the media that professionals come across in their daily routines. Indeed, there is no need to make a special effort to locate information of this nature. Newspapers, magazines, professional publications, books, and reports are all full of stories and articles on this subject. Out of all this, a pattern is emerging: Corporate America is in a continuous transition, with no end in sight. Economic anxiety, downsizing, "right sizing," and globalization are terms used to represent this transition in one form or other. No doubt, the

American economy has handled the current wave of transition with some degree of success. But, it is equally clear that transition is the permanent nature of economics in every country around the world.

There are also plenty of reasons for this transition and the anxiety associated with it. Open borders, free trade, and economic globalization are the frequently cited reasons for this transition process. Added to this are the end of the cold war, the restructuring of defense industries, and a lack of appropriate education aimed at easing the transition. Are these the underlying reasons, or are they merely superficial evidences that reflect a few fundamental causes? We will explore these questions, and suggest some answers in this book.

The term "global capitalism" is used to describe the access and use of capital as a resource across various geographies of the world. The principles of capitalism are presumed to prevail and expand under global capitalism. However, each nation attempts to cope with global capitalism in its own way, along the preferred national economic style prevailing within that nation. Implicit in the term "national economic style" is also the standard of living accepted or endured by individuals who live in that nation. The effects of global capitalism under the preferred national economic styles are well summarized in an article titled, "Economic Anxiety—Clinging to the Safety Net..." that appeared in *BusinessWeek*.[11]

> *What is certain is that the economic pressure from the fast-growing emerging economies will continue to challenge the First World well into the 21st century. More pain is surely ahead for workers of industrialized nations. Yet, national economic styles are unlikely to disappear. It may well be that rather than follow the Americans' lead, Europe and Japan will find a different way to serve the harsh taskmaster of global capitalism.*

(See Appendix I for excerpts from reference 11.)

The recent turbulence in the economies of the Far East may offer temporary relief from the competitive pressures facing the developed nations. However, this is unlikely. The global economy seeks resources at the lowest cost, wherever they can be found. In this respect, individual industries or companies in advanced nations could exploit these favorable resource situations in some nations in the Far East to further strengthen their positions. Those who do not pursue this lead may be left with competitive disadvantages. Thus, economic instability in the Far East will only be reflected as further keen competitive pressures between industries in the developed nations and their ability to compete with each other. Individual companies, the people managing them, and their workers are likely to feel increased deep anxiety. This anxiety and pressure, skewed unfavorably for the companies and their employees in the developed nations, is likely to persist for the next few decades.

There are several tried and true solutions proposed in the U.S., including investment in physical equipment, better training and education for the workforce, shared sacrifice by the management, lower taxes, new skills, etc.[1]

All these suggested solutions ignore two fundamental questions that face workers in all professions: What does global economy mean to my company or organization? What are the likely scenarios under which my organization will operate in a global economy, in the presence of a variety of national economic styles? These questions affect every employee, organization, and activity of a company. Too often, it would appear these are thought through and rationalized by a few successful chief executives. Instead of articulating them in clear and coherent terms to their employees, they translate them in terminology too frequently used in standard business practice—numbers, products, markets, geographic coverage, etc. This type of translation of strategic concepts into standard goals and objectives is nothing new. Indeed, corporate managers are intensely trained to pursue this approach. Successful managers are those who can define these quantitative objectives precisely and achieve them. Such quantitative and financial objectives were useful and appropriate in the days when the business was constrained to a single or a few national economic styles. Under those circumstances, employees had the opportunity and mobility to participate freely within their chosen national economic style.

The reality today is that a company can choose to perform segments of its operation under several preferred national economic styles, while the employees do not have that choice. For instance, a company could choose to conduct research in the United States, design and development in Germany, manufacturing in Korea or India, and operate worldwide using a distribution center in China. Thus, the company as an organization uses resources for various functions optimally, utilizing the best (most economically suitable) location for each of its functions while pursuing the global marketplace. It also implies that the standard of living of the people employed in each of these functions (locations) is different, based on their geography and the associated national economic style. The ability of individuals to move between functions, which once was accepted readily when the company was based in one country or few countries of comparable standards of living, is now restricted both for reasons of change in standards of living as well as political and national boundaries and limitations to move across them. Hence, companies operating under the global economy and under several national economic styles have additional constraints for their employees. Is it the role and responsibility of corporations to appreciate these constraints and articulate them to their employees? If it is their role and responsibility, how should they quantify these constraints, as they are in essence part of the strategic plan of the corporation?

These constraints, if real, need to be surfaced fully and appropriately. To recognize such reality is not to imply anything improper about any company or organization. It also does not imply that it calls for a class war. On the contrary, recognition of this reality may have profound implications in terms of our deployment of appropriate solutions at all levels.

Viewed from this perspective, tax cuts, better capital equipment, higher education, more training, and new skills take on new meanings and requirements for action. Instead of merely pursuing more tax cuts, we might be speaking of appropriate tax cuts. Instead of tax credits for higher education, we might be speaking of tax credits for higher learning of an appropriate kind. Instead of more training, we might be speaking of identifying and learning new or different skills to cope with changing needs.

In the following chapters, we will articulate the reasons that have now made it necessary for an organization or company to operate in a global marketplace in the presence of a multitude of national economic standards and systems. These reasons, to no one's surprise, are largely driven by technologies that harness information and logistics. Nevertheless, technology here does not imply merely computers and peripherals. It refers to the ability to acquire, process, disseminate, and deploy information and resources of any kind, at any location in the world at about the speed of light. In the end, organizations that manage information, logistics, and the technologies associated with them may be the only ones to achieve success. While this might be obvious to many professionals, it appears that most individuals maintain a clear separation between technologies of information, logistics, and their role in the organization and its performance versus their perception of their role in individual professional task performance. We will revisit these human aspects in the following chapters.

Recognition of impacts or changes of this nature lead to a whole new paradigm in our approach to the individual's job needs, why they are changing, and the associated needs in education, career development, training, etc. National policies compatible with these changing needs may be far more desirable than our present ad-hoc approaches for tax cuts, credit for higher education, etc.

Coping with the issues of transition, uncertainty, survival, and success in a marketplace driven by global capitalism in the midst of multitude national economic styles and economic standards also calls for a reevaluation of the social contract between employers and employees.

> *"The idea of a corporation taking on social responsibility is absolutely ridiculous," says Chrysler Chairman Robert J. Eaton. "You will simply burden industry to a point where it is no longer competitive."*[12]

The assertion that corporations should continue to be focused on their shareholder needs only, and should not take on any social responsibility, implies that nothing has fundamentally changed in the capitalistic style of economics, except that the marketplace has become global. As stated earlier, it is not only that a manufacturer has access to customers on a global basis, but they also have access to resources worldwide, especially human resources. These human resources are not all available under the same economic rules. Instead, these resources are available under different national economic styles. The choice or preference for these resources is also determined by the economics or standards of living, which vary throughout the world. How can any entrepreneur claim to use the rules of capitalism in managing an enterprise, while utilizing resources—particularly human resources—selected from geographies subject to the constraints of communism, socialism, socialistic capitalism, and capitalism?

This social conflict, engendered by global capitalism, has resulted in calls for a "stakeholder economy," where a company's employees, customers, and communities enjoy legislated rights. However, legislated solutions are not the preferences of Americans, who are leery of any regulatory intervention.[12]

> *And so, in isolated pockets of Corporate America, a middle path is slowly emerging, one that reflects a new paradigm for business and society in a global market. It recognizes that job security died with the 1980s—but concedes, too, that employers bear an obligation to help*

workers through transitions. And it attempts to align the interests of investors, managers, and employees, aiming to share both the risks and the rewards of doing business.

Let us reflect on this emerging paradigm. If I am an employee, I am responsible in part for the profits and losses of the company. I am also responsible for the strategic plan, operational details, product development strategy, pricing, manufacturing, sourcing, sales, distributions, etc. But how can a company function if every individual demands a role and responsibility in every aspect of the company's profitability? On the other hand, how can a company legitimately deny access and participation to all its employees, if the employees are all responsible for the overall profitability of their company or unit, in addition to carrying out their individual task or job assignments? While this appears to be an irreconcilable conflict, in reality it may not be. Indeed, a resolution to this conflict is possible. Any corporation that finds a logical approach to address these questions will be successful in the new global capitalism. We shall review possible options in the following chapters.

There are several variations proposed for the new paradigm of stakeholder economy.[12]

Pay cuts are preferred to layoffs, so that there is a shared sacrifice during business downturns. Employers are encouraged to train their employees for new skills, so that they can get work elsewhere. While employees are told that they are responsible for their own career planning and development, employers are encouraged to offer resources for self-evaluation and training.

The above solutions pose their own internal contradictions. Shared sacrifice in one form or another implies a lowering of the standard of living. Should the goal of a company be innovation and development for growth that accommodates or evens out the impact of downturn, or should the company accept downturns as an irreconcilable reality and prepare their employees for a lower standard of living through wage sharing?

What, if any, are the strategies that can make a company immune to business downturns and continue to seek constant growth in the standard of living of their employees? Are there new opportunities for such strategies in a global economy? What is the nature of training and skills that employees must possess in such a dynamic, constantly progressive company? When a company can identify and train their employees for such skills, then it is in the company's long-term interest, rather than merely a social responsibility.

This need to learn the approaches to ease the pain of transition appears to be mandatory for every company that participates in the global capitalism. For instance:

> *It has happened before: Unionism and ever-expanding regulation were the products of earlier bouts with economic anxiety, of a sense that the shareholder/stakeholder balance was out of whack. Now, Americans say they would favor tax incentives to reward employers that preserve or create jobs. What they really want is for companies to ease the pain of transition and share in the sacrifices required. Far better for employers to figure that out on their own.*[12]

In the following chapters, we will explore the fundamental causes that drive global capitalism. Understanding these causes will lead to strategies for business development. Such strategies require certain skills on the part of employees. A definite change in the outlook of the employers, in terms of human resource management, job descriptions, career development, etc., is also required. They may require some alterations in our accounting procedures as well. But all of these will be governed by the employer/employee relationship not much different from what we are familiar with in the industrial world.

There will, however, be a need for a fundamental distinction between what we call "jobs" today and what we will call them in the future. The success of the industrial world is largely due to strict division of a problem into individual tasks or assignments and a comprehensive rank ordering of the same. This is called "division of labor." It would appear that under global capitalism such task-oriented assignments or jobs may be eliminated by "solution oriented" job functions at all levels. What are task-oriented assignments? How did we get there? Why did they work? Why don't they work now? How do we know they don't work? What do we need to replace such task-oriented jobs? We shall address these questions in the following chapters.

This book will make the argument that future jobs will be more "solution oriented." Then what is a solution? What are the problems requiring solution? How does one identify or define them? How does an organization, which is based on a hierarchy of tasks, transform itself into an organization with a hierarchy of problems and their resolution? If the problem is the same from top to bottom, couldn't the hierarchy then imply changes in the scale or magnitude of the problem addressed?

In such an organization—from the top person to the lowest level employee—everyone is engaged in efforts to solve the same problem, each varying, based on their position, in the scale or magnitude of impact. We will attempt to show that such an organization is more than conceptual. Such an organization and the employees trained to perform in such an organization are very much in need. Transition to such an industrial organization is perhaps the biggest challenge for the employees. Transition to the skills required to function in the new organization is the challenge faced by all of us working in industry today. The transition process may be a collective evolution of why we carry out a given industrial activity (strategy of the company) and how we carry out the same (employment or job functions) as individuals. In this transition process, there may not be a distinction or separation between the employer's responsibility to employees and vice versa. Instead, this may be a collective transition process that, when accomplished, retains and improves the success of the company and the standard of living of the employees.

This transition may not occur at a national level. For instance, today we speak of a buoyant economy in the United States, a down-turn in Japan, slow recovery in Europe, an economic collapse in East Asia, and steady growth in India or China. These are largely linked to the national economic style, as discussed earlier. In the future we may speak of successful industrial enterprises, irrespective of their geographic location. These industrial enterprises will span global markets, utilizing appropriate resources across different national economic systems. These successful enterprises will be individual companies that have accomplished the transition collectively with their employees on a worldwide basis.

Technology, manufacturing, product/market management, and organizational structures are some of the tools being looked at to achieve this transition. Transitions in technology are not an easy challenge. An article titled, "Know When Incremental Change Will No Longer Do," reports:[13]

> *Studying development patterns in technologies ranging from typewriters to computer, MIT management and engineering professor, James Utterback, is struck by a pattern. The degree to which powerful competitors not only resist innovative threats, but actually resist all efforts to understand them, preferring to further entrench their positions in the older products. This results in a surge of productivity and performance that may take the old technology to unheard of heights. But in most cases, this is an impending death.*
>
> *This is not entirely shortsightedness: Jumping from a tired horse to a fresh one without missing a gallop is something you would prefer done by a stunt double. The old technology is still where everything you have gotten is, particularly your income, and suddenly disrupting the process makes no one happy—not stockholders, not employ-*

ees, and not customers. Keeping on with the old makes sense to a point. Guessing when you have reached that point is a big part of the trick.

The above observations in the management of technology raise several questions. Why do we need many campaigns or strategic initiatives? Is it because of our traditional approach to segmentation of tasks? Should future campaigns be multifaceted and multidimensional? This could imply that instead of a staircase approach with a series of linear or incremental accomplishments, there is an integrated or multifaceted approach to management of strategies, technologies, and core competencies. This implies a belief in the assumption that the whole is larger than some of the parts. What is this integrated approach for assessment of technology or core competency of an organization? What is the integrated approach that fosters the core competencies or the strategic underpinning of an organization in a multifaceted or multidimensional manner, almost through a parallel processing approach instead of a sequential or incremental and cumulative process? We will address several of these questions in the following chapters.

Similar issues also arise in our transition in the development and management of manufacturing for the future. A year-long study by 500 representatives of U.S. industries and their trade associations, academic researchers, and government officials, was carried out under a project titled, "The Next Generation Manufacturing Project." According to its report, "Manufacturing must be addressed as a holistic and dynamic system that integrates people, business processes and technology."[2]

This report calls for six areas targeted for change:
- Customer relationships that cultivate collaboration with customers, which permits an ability to anticipate changes in customer demands.
- Flexible manufacturing that permits reconfiguration of physical plants and facilities to accommodate short production runs and rapid changeovers.

- Workforce issues, which focus on methods to motivate workers, recognizing each individual's creativity and contribution as an essential element of the success of the enterprise as a whole.
- Strategy and tactics that permit thinking on a global scale while acting as tacticians on a local scale.
- Teamwork and partnering with anyone offering solutions for customers that goes far beyond the limits of the physical product.
- Business redefinition that constantly seeks to redefine core competencies and the company itself as the customer demand shifts.

The above conclusions raise several questions. If manufacturing must be addressed as a holistic and dynamic system, how does one define a "manufacturing system"? How does one recognize it as holistic? What are the attributes, parameters, or descriptions of a holistic manufacturing system?

Is there an organized methodology to develop customer relationships? How does it differ from traditional approaches? Can one anticipate changes with customers solely through relationships? Is there other more science or engineering based criteria that one can rely on?

What is the use of flexibility in a manufacturing environment, when the product need itself is in question? Are we talking about flexibility in production equipment, or flexibility in production processes that can meet a stream of end use patterns?

What is new, unique, or different about the work force issues of motivation and encouraging creativity? Haven't these been the key considerations all along? What is new and different in the current workplace or the future workplace?

What does thinking on a global scale mean? Can one meet global strategies by being a local tactician?

What does going "beyond the physical limits of the product" mean? How far can one go in this direction?

Many of these questions are intertwined with the central issue of operating in a global marketplace, in the presence of a multitude of national economic styles and economic standards. Yet, in the daily world, an engineering professional rarely pays attention to them, often delegating these types of questions to managers! This kind of pondering may well be the responsibility of the individual professionals. Organizations, companies, and social planners should ponder these questions as well.

Similar issues exist in the areas of product development and market development under global capitalism. In an editorial entitled, "Smaller is Replacing Bigger in Business," the following is noted:

> *Amid all the changes going on in American business, it's very easy to miss one of the most pervasive and far reaching. Nothing is having a more profound effect on the shape of finishing job shops and other companies today than the concept, "small."*
>
> *The concept of small is particularly pertinent when it comes to marketing. What many companies are thinking about is a multiple niche approach. This is not niche marketing either. For many years, companies have done their best to find the right niche for their products or service.*
>
> *Multiple niche marketing is quite different. It is based on the premise of speaking clearly and directly to the customer and recognizes that there may not be many customers in any one group or mini-niche.*
>
> *All this makes a dramatic change in our thinking today; consumers are becoming specific, individual, identifiable real people and companies. It is another way of saying that small is big today.*[14]

The points addressed in the above editorial may well be applicable to any industrial sector or group of industries. The concept that the large marketplace of yesterday is composed of multiple niche markets is frequently found to be true. This market niche may exist due to geography, customer preferences, competitive alternatives, etc. It would appear paradoxical that we find niche markets becoming the trend, when we simultaneously speak of the global marketplace and operating across multiple geographies simultaneously.

At an organizational level, everyone tends to their little garden in their back yard, while corporations depend on huge farms for their collective efficiency, productivity, and profitability. How can these extremely opposite needs be managed simultaneously? The inability to cope with this new paradox at an individual level, as well as an organization at various levels, is the unease in our transition described earlier. Computers are intended as a solution for this transition. Some might argue that computers are the cause of this transition and the associated unease. Later, we will discuss the fact that the computer is neither the cause, nor is it the solution. Instead, a fundamental change in our outlook and market perception may be necessary. How can we serve the market under the new paradigm of global capitalism? We will discuss these aspects of transition in product/market management in the chapters that follow.

Finally, how we work as individuals in an organization is in question. Here is a case in point. In an article entitled, "Let's Work Concurrently," it is stated:

> *Business is constantly challenged to find ways to do things quicker, cheaper and better and not just here, but all over the world. Major vehicle elements can't be viewed individually anymore and designers can no longer pass engineering concepts over the wall to manufacturing. Engineers and managers must function as one cohesive unit from concept through manufacture.*
>
> *Although the necessity for concurrent or simultaneous engineering has been recognized for a long time, the thinking of manufacturing and design engineer has not reflected that shift. Manufacturing engineers strive to come up with the best competitive, innovative manufacturing process in the world, while product engineers' goal is the most creative, eye-catching design in the world.*[15]

The article continues to suggest that in order to achieve the intended results in this global, competitive economy, it is necessary for marketing, product design, and manufacturing people to work concurrently from the beginning to the end of any project. It is also suggested that these key players work together as a team with no barriers and with effective communication. Indeed, to this effect, intense training is provided on team building and communication skills. These training programs get very detailed at times to include such special skills as how to conduct effective meetings.

The intent of everyone in Corporate America to work as a team and communicate effectively is equalled in no other part of the world. If intent is a measure of success, Corporate America need not fear. Yet, success does not necessarily come readily to those who work effectively as part of a team. For example, a friend of mine who is a good engineer recently told me that she had to find another job, as she has been "reengineered." This is one of the recommendations of the team where she was the leader!

What is the purpose of the team? How is it linked with the purpose of the company? These are the questions neglected in the rush to transition to the global economy. A team is often driven by one or a few objectives. If the objectives are clear, then why do we need the redundancies of all team members participating in a project from beginning to end? Is it because the team members come with a mindset to execute a task rather than solve a problem? Do we need interdisciplinary team effort, or are we seeking interdisciplinary thought processes in individuals? Are we seeking integration of individual tasks without redundancies, or are we seeking an integrated problem-solving approach, where everyone individually contributes with the responsibility of a common purpose all the time? In that approach can individuals strictly adhere to specific tasks as their goals and objectives? When a problem is divided into tasks, does it not automatically create separations and boundaries between tasks? How does one create an organization where individuals are aligned to the goal of solving the problem, no matter what it takes? Such an organization will be distinctly different from one where individuals are aligned to tasks that collectively lead to problem resolution, but only at the cost of severe internal redundancies and friction. What makes such problem resolution oriented organizations possible or practical today?

The series of questions raised in this chapter are a natural outcome of our attempt to answer the following: "How can an organization or company manage the transitions into global capitalism, while operating under multinational economic styles and their associated economic standards of living?" Along with the issues facing the organization are a series of questions that individual professionals need to confront. Many of the questions raised here are addressed in subsequent chapters with an attempt to provide a clear and coherent strategy to succeed. As we will see, this strategy—which we will call the "System Approach"—offers the key to survival in the new global economy.

Chapter 2
Global Economy— Separating the Myths from Reality

Comprehending the global competitive environment and how to deal with it is not just a societal issue for academics, professionals, and managers. It is a personal issue of concern to every individual. Along with the preparation of companies and organizations for the future, there is also a need for every individual to prepare for their future, and the future of their children. In the previous chapter we concluded that the underlying cause of the modern global competitive environment is global capitalism along with prevailing national economic styles. It is valuable to explore the factors that lead to global capitalism.

Global competitiveness implies that for every economic activity, everyone involved in it needs to have a competitive advantage over resources available anywhere in the world. An article, published in *The Herald Tribune* on January 27, 1898 (over a hundred years ago) states,[18]

1898: Economic Boom

New York—The National Manufacturers Association held its annual meeting in New York today (Jan. 27). All members agreed that there was a boom in business, which would steadily increase. Not only has domestic business gone forward with rapid strides, but also foreign demand for American products has increased. The return of confidence, due to the good crops and the settlement of the tariff, are accepted as the causes of the vast improvement in the country's commercial condition.

This news item published over 100 years ago discusses sales across international boundaries and the constraints on those sales in the form of tariffs imposed by individual nations. Such tariffs are nothing more than an exercise to implement the chosen economic policy of that nation. Buying and selling of goods across national borders is also not a new development. Merchants have traded goods between nations since the beginning of recorded history. As international trade has progressed and intensified over the centuries, the regulation of sales between nations through the use of tariffs and other restrictions has been an integral part of such trade. In most cases, this type of trade between nations involved finished goods manufactured within a single geography. Thus, all engineering and economic activity associated with the manufacture of the "product" generally remained within the boundaries of one nation.

Even though trading across national boundaries generally centered on finished goods or "end products," the exception to this was the shipment of raw materials, largely due to their source of availability. The concept of "globalization" was born when subassemblies and components were moved across the national boundaries. Use of small engines made in Japan to be integrated into small cars manufactured in the U.S. is a case in point. The initial reason for such transnational movement of components or subassemblies was largely driven by technology. The demands for small cars far outpaced the ability of engineering teams to design, manufacture, and qualify small engines in the U.S. within the time required. This prompted large manufacturers to import small engines to be assembled in their cars which were manufactured in Detroit. As technology progressed in all parts of the world, there was an equilibrium reached in the manufacture and shipment of small engines across the geographies of the world.

As time progressed and the national economies changed, it was possible to manufacture and ship components instead of subassemblies across the geographies. Instead of an industrial world consisting of a few countries in Europe and the U.S., several countries, most notably Japan, emerged and became centers of engineering and manufacturing activities. Developments of this nature gradually increased the movement of subassemblies and components across the national boundaries (Figure 2.1.a & b). The complexities of these interconnections between nations increased as more of them became viable candidates largely based on technological excellence, labor cost advantages, and/or national economic standards (Figure 2.1.c). While information systems have been partly responsible for this progression, the majority of these developments were due to the global logistic capabilities of individual companies.

Throughout this process, the engineering functions were largely confined to one or a few locations and were generally unaffected. The manufacturing activities, however, were distributed over many locations, largely influenced by labor costs. Frequently, the manufacturing locations were also displaced or redistributed for reasons of quality. Such quality factors were generally a reflection of consistent work practices at the manufacturing locations. This was the period of severe layoffs for blue-collar workers in the U.S. Not surprisingly, this is also the beginning of a period of over 20 years of gradual decline in real income for most Americans.

Real wages have been falling for the bottom 60% of American males at 0.8% a year for the last 20 years. In

30 • The System Approach

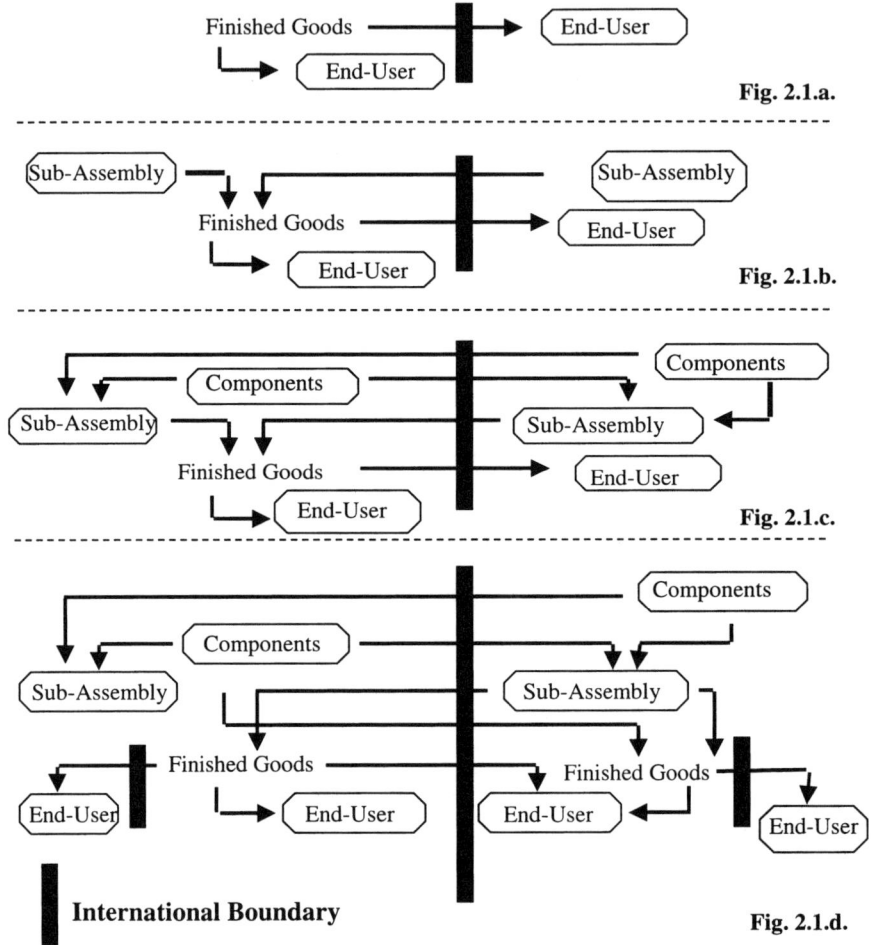

Figure 2.1 • Progressive expansion in the use of "global logistics" in the manufacture of components to finished goods.

any one-year you don't notice anything. But since 1975, it has meant a nearly 20% drop in purchasing power for a large number of people.[19]

As time progressed, the collection, processing, and exchange of information between locations could occur at about the speed of light, thanks to telephone, fax, electronic data transfer, and finally network (intranet and internet) capabilities.

This resulted in the deployment of a new core competence, which we will call "information automation." In due course global logistics and information automation became almost inseparably intertwined. This gave birth to a new dimension in the management of engineering activities.

Engineering functions, which were generally concentrated in a few locations, were now distributed worldwide in several strategically selected locations. Redundancies in engineering activities between locations could be reduced and often eliminated altogether. A few engineers in selected locations could carry out the functions of entire engineering departments by appropriately communicating through electronic media and occasionally traveling between locations. This was the beginning of the impact of information technology on white-collar labor. (See Figure 2.2.)

Beginnings of the impact of information automation on the white-collar labor force can be traced to as early as 1950s when as many as forty keypunch operators could be eliminated in accounting or payroll departments by the acquisition of a single computer. Computer Numerical Control, which began as a means to manipulate individual areas of a machine tool, has today emerged as a means to manage information for a variety of purposes. In reality, it is better described as the elimination of the tasks of information collection, exchange, and processing, replaced by means of information automation.

The pervasive nature of task-oriented engineering activities focused on information collection, exchange, or processing can be better visualized in Figure 2.3.[20] It shows the concurrent engineering activities and flow of information, and how all aspects of the process can be managed using computers and appropriate software. It is not the intent here to discuss concurrent engineering in detail. There are several excellent books on this topic. What is important for our present analysis is to visualize every job, each of which is, in reality, an assignment to collect, exchange, or process information. It must be recognized that the tools of information automation,

32 • The System Approach

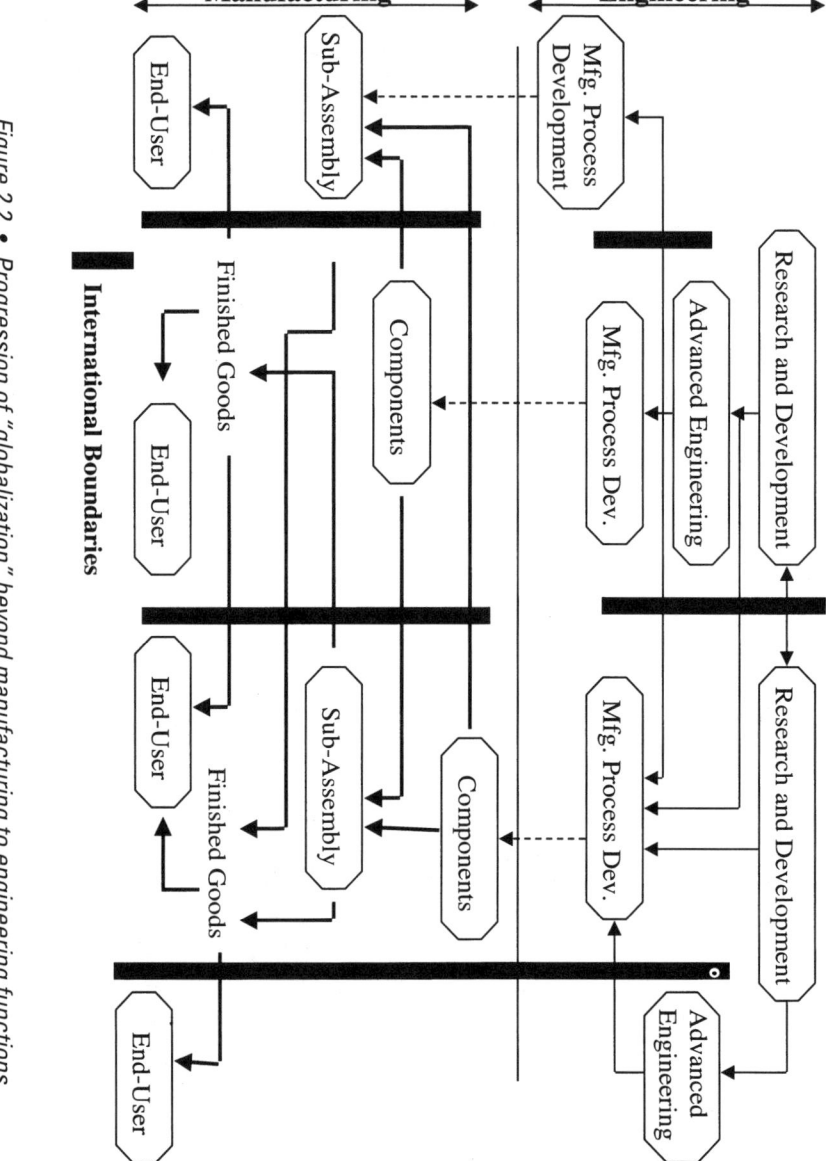

Figure 2.2 • Progression of "globalization" beyond manufacturing to engineering functions.

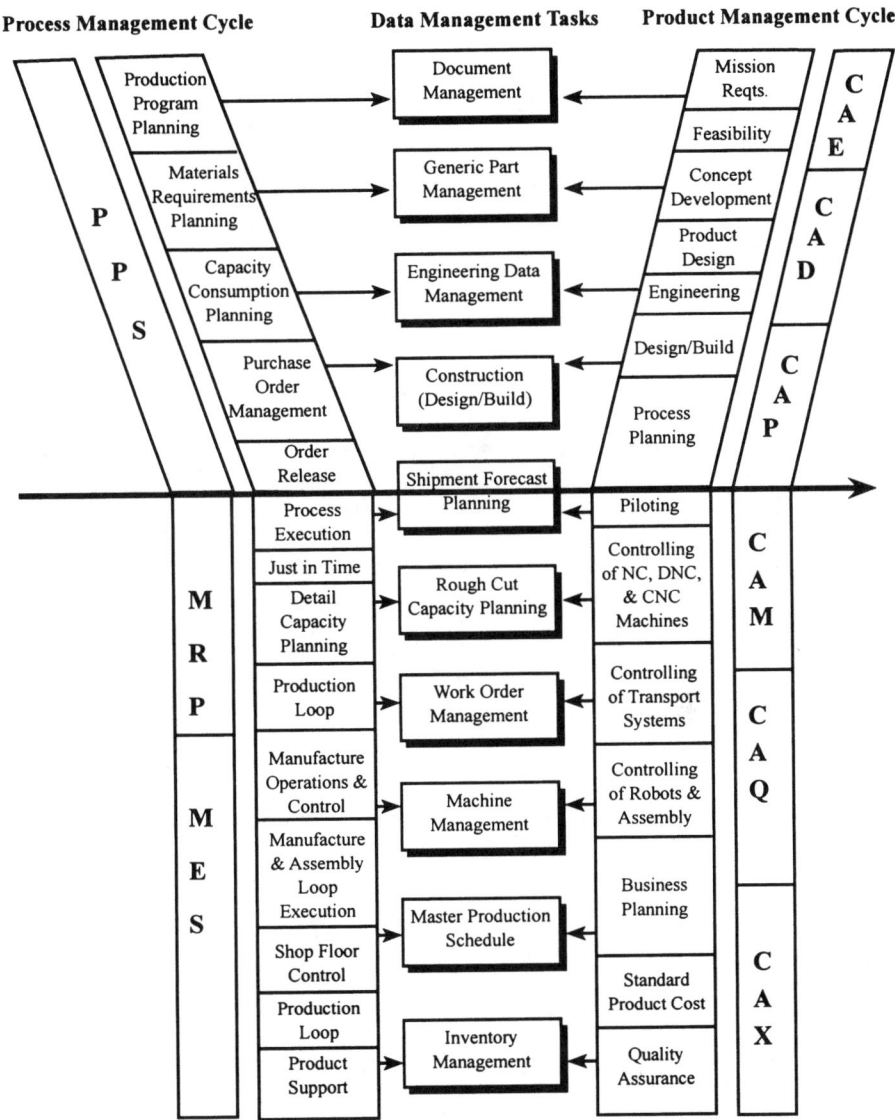

Figure 2.3 • Series of computer based tools for "information automation."[20]

such as computer-based systems and the associated software, can perform the same tasks. This is evidenced by successful implementation of computer systems for shop flow control, such as material requirement planning and processing in the manufacturing operation. This logical process is now being extended to activities preceding manufacturing, such as design and product/process development functions.

Now look at the evolution of globalization from another perspective. Every industrial activity—indeed for that matter any activity—can be conceived of as an "input/process/output" system. Stated in another way, activity is the means that transforms a certain set of inputs into outputs that have a useful purpose. This description of any activity is illustrated in Figure 2.4.a. In order to execute the activity, it is necessary to bring together or transfer the inputs of any kind into the process. Similarly, it is easy to visualize a set of transfer events to deliver the outputs of the process. Every event at the input, process, and output stage of the activity, along with the transfer events, carries with it information pertinent to that stage of the industrial activity. As a result, any industrial activity can be conceived of as an "input/process/output" system with a large group of events, each requiring collection, processing, and/or dissemination of information or transfer events involving physical objects.

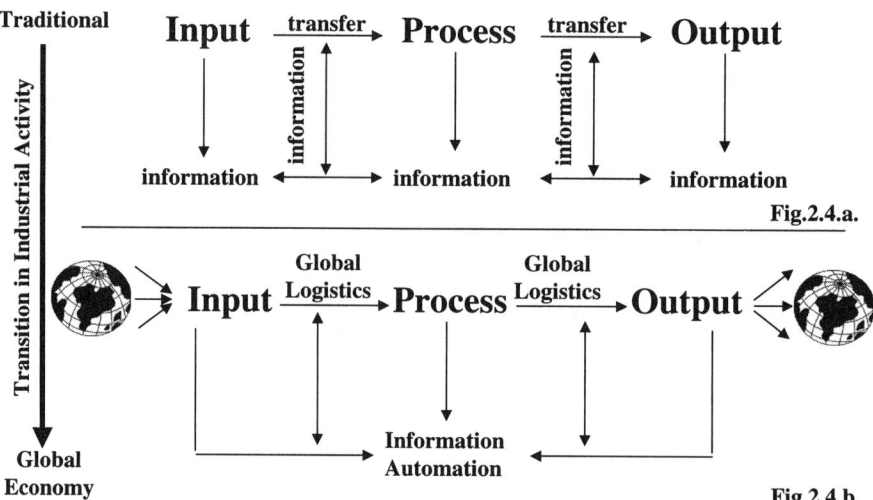

Figure 2.4 • Transition in industrial activity from traditional to global economy.

In a traditional industrial society, each of these events consisted of a "task" or a "job." These jobs may be blue-collar in nature, which usually involve physical transfer of objects and their relative positioning. They were white-collar in nature if they involved events pertaining to information collection, processing, and dissemination. In this scenario, it is easy to recognize functions such as administration, supervision, and management in every area of industrial activity such as Human Resources, Accounting, Purchasing, Sales Administration, Customer Service, Manufacturing, Engineering, Research, etc. All of these involve large groups of tasks involving collection, processing, and dissemination of information. All these tasks or jobs are candidates for replacement by tools of information automation.

In addition to automation related to information at a given location, it is also now possible to utilize such tools for enhancing the logistics—or transfer events—on a worldwide basis. Let us explore this through a simple example. Consider an automotive subassembly manufacturer in Gloucester, England, that sources their components from a manufacturer in Cleveland, Ohio. Just a few years ago, if one of the engineers in Gloucester needed to make certain design changes in a component in order to enhance the functional effectiveness of the subassembly, this would have required a drawing to be drafted and sent physically (by mail or courier) to the engineering department of the manufacturer in Cleveland. The number of steps involved and the time consumed in this scenario are obvious.

Today, we are all aware that an identical transfer of concept to commercial order, with a few revision steps included, can be accomplished within a few hours. Indeed, such exploration of options and alternatives could have involved as many companies as might be needed on a worldwide basis. The same can be said of the effectiveness of information automation and global logistics on the output side of the process and on a worldwide basis. Thus, industrial activity in the past consisted of an input/process/output system that contained

36 • The System Approach

a collection or multitude of tasks and was carried out on a local basis. In the global economy all industrial activities, while retaining the same input/process/output system, have also transitioned into a cluster of competencies transforming resources (inputs) from anywhere in the world to outputs to be utilized anywhere in the world. (Figure 2.4.b.) The transformation engine continues to be technology. However, in a global economy the technology of any industrial process is integral with two other core competencies, global logistics and information automation. Such a global enterprise is a transformer of inputs from worldwide sources through a cluster of three core competencies to outputs serving worldwide users. This concept of a global enterprise as an input/process/output system is shown in Figure 2.5.

As a result of this transition, a large number of white-collar (engineering) jobs are being eliminated. In every instance the jobs lost are those that are task-oriented, primarily involving collection, exchange, or processing of information. Of

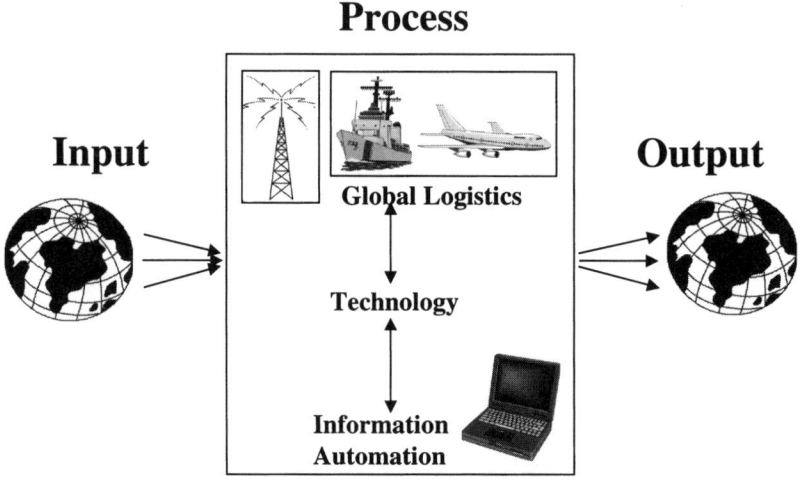

Figure 2.5 • *Global economy: Where industrial activities of individuals, organizations or the enterprise can all be represented as input/process/output transformation activities governed by their capabilities in technology, information automation, and global logistics for utilizing resources from anywhere in the world and to serve the worldwide end-user needs.*

course, there is a new need for people who establish the procedures and processes for such information automation. These employees are called software engineers and systems engineers. There has been significant growth in these jobs, especially in companies dealing with computer-oriented tasks. But the growth, which results from the elimination of labor in information collection, exchange, and processing tasks, is not large enough to offset the loss of the jobs they have eliminated. Otherwise, there would be no net gain to industrial productivity.

Successful industries must and will implement productivity improvements from every possible and appropriate source. This is the natural law of business economics. But when engineers function without understanding of the laws of economics, or managers do not translate the laws of economics in terms that make sense for engineers, then all the myths associated with globalization come into play.

Let us look at this transition in human terms. Every engineer can look at his job function and ask the questions, "What is my job? Is it only related to information collection, exchange, or processing? Is it related merely to transfer events or logistics?" For example, a design as conceived by an engineer is knowledge. Translation of this knowledge into a drawing—the job of drafting—is merely an information processing activity, amenable to automation.

The engineer could ask two more questions:
- "What percentage of my job is focused on information collection, exchange, or processing?" The larger this percentage, the better the likelihood that such a job will be replaced with tools of information automation.
- "How many identical jobs exist in my organization?" Multiple tasks, carried out in identical fashion, either related to information or to transfer events, are ideal candidates for productivity improvement through tools of information automation and global logistics.

Answers to the above questions in realistic terms will provide a logical basis for predicting potential job uncertainty in the transition from the traditional to the global economy. This should not be cause for panic or despair. Analysis of this kind will lead to ways and means to proactively reduce the tasks involved in individual jobs and replace them with additional value added functions for the company.

We can conclude that globalization has three aspects that have impact on individuals, organizations, companies, and industries. Restated, these are:
- Technology and its excellence,
- Global logistics, permitting the use of technology anywhere through sourcing of intellectual or engineering resources, as well as physical resources, components, and subassemblies, on a worldwide basis, and
- Information automation, which increases the efficiency in the collection, processing, and dissemination of information, in turn increasing the efficiency of deploying technology and global logistics.

Extended to the limits, these three capabilities can allow a company to operate on a 24-hour basis with resources deployed throughout a borderless world. Few companies have reached this ultimate capability. Yet, many are progressing in this direction. Even as we write, there are companies that have their research and development functions in the U.S., engineering in Europe, process development in Japan, and manufacturing operations in East Asia, serving the worldwide market. This is perhaps just a small example of what is yet to come. Such a global enterprise driven by a set of three core competencies is illustrated in Figure 2.5.

All of these forces are bringing about radical revisions in job functions, and changes in the nature and types of employment available in various locations in the world. They also have profound impact on organizational styles. Historically, the industrial world has achieved efficiency largely through task-oriented job assignment. If the overall activity is dissected into individual components, and each individual is allowed to specialize in individual tasks, the highest proficiency can be achieved. The sum of such highly proficient, task-oriented workers results in a highly productive organization. The more complex the job, the efficiency will be greatest when the job is broken down into the smallest individual elements. This indeed is the basis of large organizations, with multitudes of job functions and several organizational layers. The invention of the assembly line for automobile manufacturing was founded on this concept of distribution of labor in the manufacturing process. The same is true for management of white-collar job functions. This type of traditional organizational alignment is shown in Figure 2.6.

Global logistics has impacted the bottom layers of the organizational pyramid, frequently referred to as the blue-collar work force. As physical resources became available on a world-

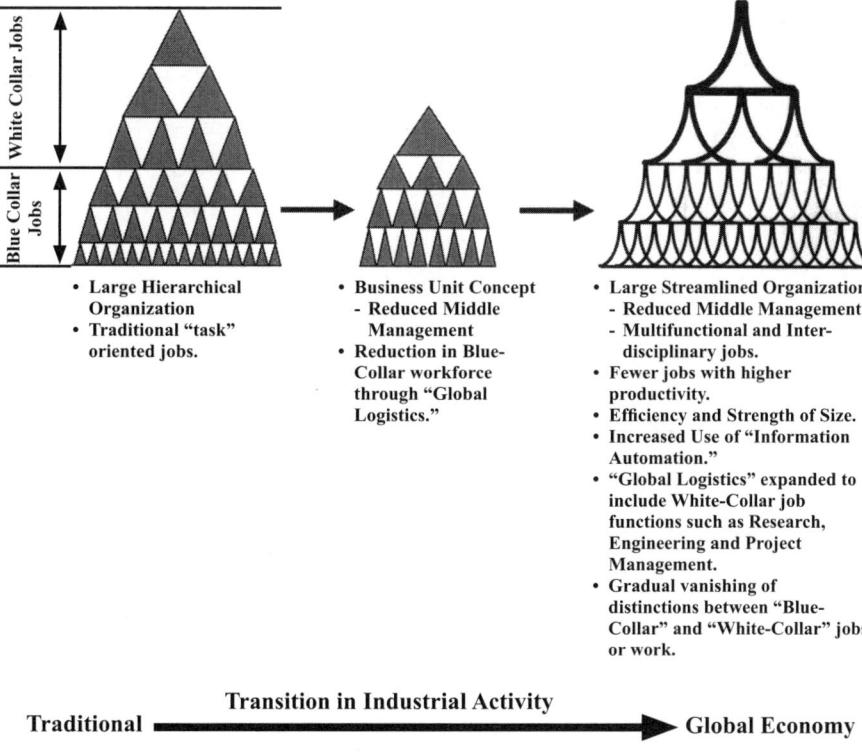

Figure 2.6 • Evolution in organizational styles and their impact on jobs and functions.

wide basis, a need for responsiveness, faster than that possible through large hierarchical organizations, has developed. In response to this, there have been several efforts to improve the efficiency and responsiveness of the upper levels of the organizational pyramid called the "white-collar workforce," and the management layers. This resulted in the "business unit" concept. (Figure 2.6.)

The business unit organization was indeed small and hence fast and flexible. It could also rely on resources from worldwide sources through global logistics. But the redundancies in the collection, processing, and deployment of information also grew rapidly. Each business unit needs the same information or similar sets of information. While there was a reduction in blue-collar labor (and hence the cost), the cost of white-collar labor increased due to the redundancies required in the business unit concept. With the advent of information automation, the efficiency and responsiveness of the business unit style of organization could be retained, while simultaneously decreasing the cost of information related tasks at every level of the organization. The explosive growth in this competence may indeed be the single largest factor for the recent productivity increases in U.S. industries.

Along with this transition has been a fundamental change in the job content at every level of the organization. Jobs, which are mere "tasks" or the execution of individual events, are being replaced by total responsibility for a "problem" or an "input/process/output" system. (Figure 2.6.) In other words, individual employees are required to span across a wide range of tasks and assume larger responsibility, with a focus on deliverables of larger value/benefits to the enterprise. A global enterprise is a transformation engine taking resources from anywhere in the world. These inputs are transformed through three core competencies—technology, information automation, and global logistics—into outputs, which in turn are used to serve the needs of users on a worldwide basis. (Figure 2.5)

Another view of the global enterprise is an organization with certain characteristics that transform resources from anywhere in the world into outputs deployed anywhere in the world. Such an organization is large enough, in terms of its competence, to span a wide range of functions and responsibilities with far fewer individuals at every level and fewer levels of organizational hierarchy. The individuals in such organizations also reflect the organization as a whole, with multidimensional capabilities, problem-resolution mindsets, and the ability to deploy technology, global logistics, and information automation in a seamless fashion.

As developing nations improve their economies due to the impact of globalization, the advantages of lower labor cost is gradually shrinking. With advancements in technology and elimination of redundancies in operations, the labor cost will become even less of a significant factor. Under these conditions, blue-collar jobs also are transformed from a large pool of task-oriented workers to a smaller pool of multifunctional and interdisciplinary job assignments.

There is abundant evidence of these types of change in organizational styles and their impact on jobs and functions. The acquisition and merger of several large companies is often economically viable now, thanks to the benefits of information automation. The critical size for management of such growing large organizations is limited only by their proficiency in information automation. The merger of McDonald Douglas and Boeing is an excellent example. Similarly, manufacturing operations, once considered prohibitively expensive for labor cost reasons and hence shipped overseas, are now returning to the U.S., thanks in large part to technology advancements in manufacturing processes and the quality of labor pool necessary to carry out such operations. These labor pools are less like the blue-collar workers of the past and more closely resemble professionals or white-collar workers.

In all of these changes, noted in Figure 2.6, one aspect appears to be constant. This aspect appears to be independent of job level, from the blue-collar worker to the top executive

42 • The System Approach

of the company. Individual task-oriented job assignments are disappearing. These are being replaced by job functions that are multifunctional and interdisciplinary in nature. These job functions have a larger span of responsibility and authority. All those redundancies in job functions, which used to exist for reasons of information collection, processing, and transfer, are being eliminated through information automation. Any tasks that can be performed at lowest labor cost locations anywhere in the world are being shipped offshore. New jobs are being created that integrate technology, global logistics, and information automation. Thus, a new form of employment is emerging where every worker, instead of being responsible for executing a task, is becoming a worker responsible for solving a problem. The problem often involves simultaneous integration of tasks. Employees are required to be multifunctional in their skills. Such transition in the enterprise, as well as the job functions of the individuals, is illustrated in Figure 2.7.

The consequences of this new style of job function—problem solver versus task executor—have an impact at all levels

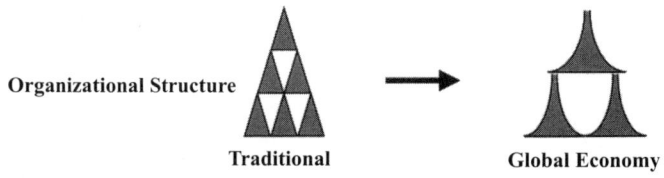

	Traditional	Global Economy
Organizational Structure		
Impact on Enterprise or Industry:		
• Organizational Layers	Many	Few
• Customer Base	Few or Limited	Large or Worldwide
• Supplier or Resource Base	Few or Limited	Large or Worldwide
• Market Segments	Few and Large	Several and "Niche"
Impact on Individuals:		
• Job Function	Task Execution	Problem Resolution
• No. of Employees	Many	Few
• Performance Expectation	Individual Contributor	Interdependent Problem Solver
• Nature of Assignments	Repetitive	Diverse
• Range of Skills Required	Narrow	Broad
• Authority or Responsibility	Small	Large
• Basis of team effort	Concurrent Engineering	Concurrency in Thought Process
• Value Addition Per Employee	Incremental	Quantum or Large Scale

Figure 2.7 • Impact on the enterprise and the individuals due to "globalization."

of the jobs within an organization. In this respect, the unease and uncertainty felt by a large cross section of the society is real, and it is here to stay. This discomfort, due to changing job functions, is best represented through the bad dream described in Chapter 1. The impact of such changes on individuals is also described through the several references cited earlier.

The globalization of any industry or enterprise leads to profound changes in organizational structures, as described in Figure 2.7. As a result, there are far fewer levels of organizational layers than ever before. Enterprises compete for markets on a worldwide basis, while simultaneously utilizing resources available worldwide. Because of this ability to access markets on a worldwide basis (due to global logistics), enterprises have the opportunity to participate in a large diversity of markets, many of which might have been previously inaccessible or ignored as niche markets. Equally important is the role of information automation, which permits handling a wide range of information in a short period of time, with greater comprehension than possible before.

Thus, excellences in global logistics and information automation are synergistic. This in turn enhances the ability of industries to pursue several market segments and create new niche markets, when required. It is important to recognize that the ability to create and service niche markets has now been enabled. This perspective is different from the view that markets, due to some strange forces of globalization, have become increasingly segmented and highly diversified and therefore unprofitable or even impossible to service.

Figure 2.7 also outlines the impact of globalization on individuals. We have discussed this in some detail earlier in this chapter. In summary, all of those job functions, which were merely there for collection, processing, and dissemination of information, are now being consolidated through advancements in technology that is focused on information automation. Further, those tasks that are largely labor intensive are being displaced from high labor cost to lower labor cost locations anywhere in the world. Such transplant of labor is made possible through means of global logistics, aided by information automation. The jobs available in the advanced economies and in the established industries are becoming fewer in number, with certain specific characteristic features. They are generally broad in their scope. The range of skills required to execute them is also broad. This is in contrast to specific, highly specialized skills that found favor in the previous narrow and task-oriented assignments. In a similar fashion, the authority or responsibility of job assignments today is rather large, with expectations of quantum improvements in performance. As a result, the individual is simultaneously part of a team with fewer members, with larger responsibility, and with greater expectations than ever before. If there ever was a "knowledge worker," as described by Peter Druker,[21] such a knowledge worker makes demands on his knowledge incessantly in today's global industry and global marketplace.

The shift in demand towards solely knowledge-oriented activities is evident to those seeking opportunities for jobs involving information collection, processing, and dissemination. Take for instance a request for information from a colleague in the early 1980s. The request had to be documented, verified, transmitted, received and reviewed. After this stage, the requested information was identified. Then there was a series of steps, just as before, in the transmission process until the requester received the information. In all of these, the initiation of the request for information (input required for a problem-solving need) and the identification of the pertinent information are the only knowledge-oriented activities. Everything else involves tasks associated with information collection, processing, and dissemination. With the means now available for information automation, all of these tasks can be automated and executed in a fraction of a second (such as the case with e-mail, database management, etc.). Thus, individuals are constantly required to contribute to knowledge-oriented activities with little time in-between. When put together in this fashion, an individual can perform as a knowledge worker with a series of instantaneous knowledge related activities interrupted for only extremely short periods between these value added activities. In this regard, the individual becomes a tireless knowledge worker, with multiple assignments that put a constant demand on time and energy. With increased efficiency in global logistics and information automation, individuals feel that demands for value added activities are occurring with greater frequency and increasing intensity.

This leaves the impression that an individual is burdened with the job of two or three people. The only way out of this dilemma is for the individual to transform from a "task-oriented" mindset to an attitude of "interdisciplinary problem solver." This requires a focus on concurrency in thought processes related to a number of core competencies, with an eye on "problem resolution." It would appear that such a problem resolution approach also requires an output or value addition of a significant or quantum nature.

At first glance, the impact of globalization on individuals would appear to be different, depending on their geographic location. In some respects, this may be true, based on factors as outlined in Table 2.1. There are several economic factors impacting an industry or enterprise. Some factors frequently cited are: cost of capital, labor cost, cost of environmental or

Table 2.1

**Influence of Geographic Factors on Industrial Enterprise
(And hence individuals employed in an enterprise)**

- **Economic**
    - Cost of Capital
    - Labor Cost
    - Environmental Cost
- **Political**
    - Industry/Government Alliances
- **Cultural**
- **Technological**
    - Incremental Improvements—Better Mouse Trap
    - Quantum Improvements—Different Mouse Trap

ecological factors, etc. These factors do vary between geographies of the world, and there are also variations in political and cultural factors, depending on geographic location.

Impacts on these variations in an enterprise or industry are diminishing rapidly under globalization. Thus, the technological factors and their impact may be the ultimate determinant, irrespective of the geographic location of the enterprise or industry. Such worldwide competitiveness, solely based on technology and irrespective of other considerations, may happen in the future. For the next few decades, however, advantages in productivity may be the competitive weapon—both for individuals as well as for the enterprise—against the economic, political, and cultural factors and their variations dependent on geography in a global economy.

Regardless of the factors selected for the competitive advantage, one needs to have an edge to be successful in any activity. This is true for individuals as well as enterprises. The ultimate advantage may be quantified in terms of productivity, value, or benefit obtained over the cost incurred for such benefit. This is schematically shown in Figure 2.8. It is the law of any industrial activity that the success of any enterprise or individual is dependent on the productivity advantage in that activity. In the past, it was sufficient to establish productivity advantages within a nation or among a few nations. Due to globalization, such advancements now are required to be achieved, considering all enterprises or individuals engaged in the same industrial activity, anywhere in the world.

The term "benchmarking" is frequently used to quantify accomplishments in productivity. Frequently benchmarking becomes complex and complicated, due to the number of parameters involved and the description of the activities as a collection of tasks. Benchmarking is sought to explain each task or activity. On the other hand, each enterprise may be thought of as an activity or process resulting in certain values or benefits to all the participants in the activity. Such value or benefit, if quantified, becomes a true measure of productivity. Then for every individual, enterprise, or industry involved in a

Global Economy—Separating the Myths from Reality • 47

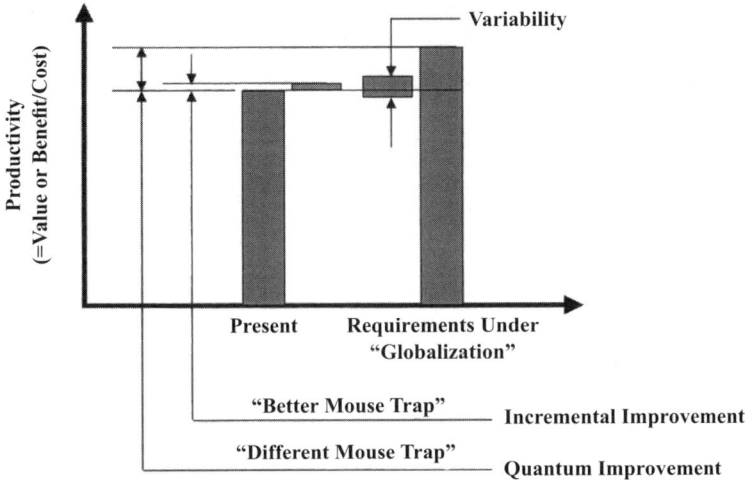

Figure 2.8 • Driven by "globalization," quantum improvement in productivity, or a "different mouse trap" is the expectation in the output of individuals, organizations, or the enterprise.

process, the productivity should be measured in terms of the same value or benefit achieved by the process.

Globalization requires constant striving to improve productivity (Figure 2.8). If productivity improvements are incremental, it is difficult to identify the benefit of such improvements. Frequently, such incremental improvements may get lost in the "noise" or variability in measurements. The noise becomes larger as the factors and their measurements are considered on a worldwide basis. On the other hand, if the productivity improvements are large or quantum in nature and such advantage can be perceived on a worldwide basis, then such individual or enterprise remains successful in a global economy.

Success in a global economy—for any enterprise—requires the following analysis:
- Are there approaches or strategies that help to define the activity of the enterprise in terms of an input/process/output system with its associated value or benefit to the participants in the system?

- Once the input/process/output system is defined, are there approaches to achieve quantum improvement in the output of such systems?

From the above analysis, a set of conclusions may be drawn from the point of view of individual employees, such as:
- There is a profound change in the workplace. Task-oriented job functions are being eliminated and replaced by fewer solution oriented jobs.
- This change is occurring at all levels—from the lowest level worker to the highest executive in the organization.
- This diminishing employment opportunity can be managed through shared sacrifice, thereby lowering the living standard of all involved.
- Alternatively, those few that find the means or ability to transition to the problem solver role or job function survive and succeed in the changing employment marketplace.
- These problem solvers are often described as entrepreneurial, system oriented, holistic, or ultrapreneurs.

It is worthwhile quoting two examples here to make the point. In an industrial manufacturing operation, several process steps and operations were eliminated or replaced by a set of five CNC machine tools forming a cell. The single operator in charge of this cell was proficient in machine operations, CNC programming, production planning, and optimizing the capacity utilization. To recognize his achievement, this blue-collar worker's job title was changed to Asset Manager with a ceremonial white coat to indicate the transition process.

In the July 7, 1997 issue of *IndustryWeek*[3], a new breed of executives is described as "ultrapreneurs." In essence, these ultrapreneurs characterize the problem solvers. It is noted in the referenced article that the ultrapreneurs get twice the work done in one work hour as other executives, and their work is better and more productive. While the article places ultrapreneurs in the executive categories, one can note that such traits are the sure signs for success at any level in the organization. Such traits are also the expectation of the successful organizations, as well as successful enterprises in a global economy. This is schematically illustrated as the "different mouse trap" in Figure 2.8.

- Thus the "stakeholder economy" is perhaps a restatement of the changing scenarios in job functions from one of executing a "task" and getting paid for it, to one of "solving a problem" and the reward occuring only when the "problem" is solved. In this respect, the opportunity for reward arises as a result of "problem resolution" for everyone involved and invariant of the level of the job in the organization.
- Such "problem resolution" orientation brings with it job assignments that are multidisciplinary in nature. Thus, a "task"-oriented individual may shift between companies, that require specific skills. This may appear as having to incur "several career changes in one life time." However, the "problem solver" may shift between tasks within a given company. As long as the "problem" exists, the "problem solver" has job security that may bring greater longevity in a job versus a task-oriented individual. Alternately, the employee is required to frame the "problem" in the context of the needs of his/her enterprise, and then solve them to deliver the desired value/benefits.
- "Problem resolution" oriented individuals by nature become interdisciplinary in their efforts and in their approach to problem solving. The enormous need for "team building" efforts may simply be an evidence of force fitting "task"-oriented individuals and thought processes into an interdisciplinary "problem resolution" oriented need.
- If "interdisciplinary problem solving" skills are indeed required in the jobs of today and tomorrow, how can such job functions be identified, formulated, or developed? What is the nature of education required for such skills or capabilities? What changes are needed in our infrastructure—organization, procedures, and policies—that will facilitate development of people for such newly needed skills?
- Any incentives and national investments—such as tax credits for education, etc.—may be more effective if they

address the above changes in the workplace and take them into account. This may, for instance, imply a rethinking on the nature of education and training. Support for more education of a kind that fosters "task"-orientation may be of no value or benefit, if analytical thinking and "problem solving" skills are really the need.

We will explore some of the above questions with possible approaches for the transition from task orientation to problem resolution. The methodology for such transition is the "System Approach," which we shall develop in detail in the next few chapters.

Chapter 3
The System Approach

Industrial enterprises are composed of many organizations. Traditionally, these organizations may be identified as R&D, engineering, manufacturing, marketing, sales and service, etc. Interconnecting organizations may also be observed within an enterprise such as accounting, human resources, legal, etc. In the past, several of these organizations have been aligned or combined into entities called business units. The recent trend is to merge such organizations and create cross-functional teams. In every one of these alignments, an enterprise may be perceived of as a collection or integration of organizations. Every one of these organizations, in turn, is comprised of unit processes or individual functions. Every organization may be perceived as a unique combination of unit processes. Employees in any industrial activity may be responsible for unit processes, organizations, or enterprises depending on their job function. Every activity of any individual, organization, enterprise, or industry can be treated as an input/process/output sequence as shown in Figure 3.1.

Every process has certain inputs. The industrial activity involves the process of transforming the "inputs" into "outputs," or benefits of value to the customer. When described in this fashion, the immediate question will be: What is the process that I, as an individual, am involved in? The question could also be: What is the process that my organization, company, enterprise, or industry, is involved with? The clearer the comprehension of the process, the better defined is the description of our problem, job, organization, enterprise, industry, etc.

At this point, the reader may wish to define the process with which he/she is involved. In other words, answer the question: What is my job? The same question can be asked by the lowest level employee as well as the highest executive of a company or industry. In the traditional economy, the answer to this question varies depending on the assigned task. In the

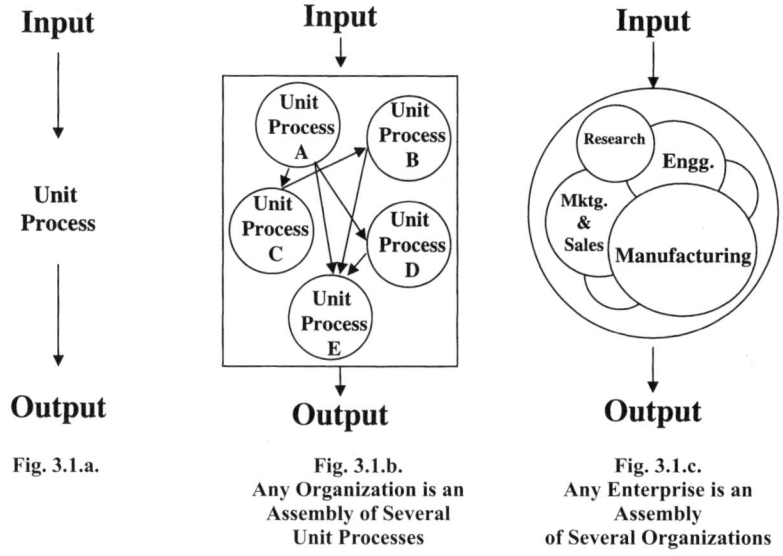

Fig. 3.1.a.

Fig. 3.1.b.
Any Organization is an Assembly of Several Unit Processes

Fig. 3.1.c.
Any Enterprise is an Assembly of Several Organizations

Figure 3.1 • *The enterprise is an assembly of organizations. Organizations are composed of unit processes. Individuals participate in the process at every level based on the job function (or the size and scope of the "system" responsibility).*

global economy, the answer becomes the same at every level in an organization or enterprise, and results in a description of a uniform process. (Figure 3.2.a.) Everyone in an enterprise is then required to be focused on achieving quantum improvements in the productivity of the deployment of nearly the same process. The consistency in the definition of the process across individuals and their organization, and across the several organizations of any enterprise, may be an essential determinant for success of any enterprise or industry in the global economy.

Lacking clear definitions or common language of the process, the job functions of individuals and the activity of the enterprise frequently become more and more like a black box (Figure 3.2.b). Those few who can achieve significant improvements for their enterprises are treated with reverence worthy of a magician. These miracle workers are frequently recognized when the traditional output measures of the process are well established and easily identified. Traditional output measures are frequently described in terms of the financial performance of the enterprise or industry. The significant improvements in financial performance are treated with respect and due recognition. In the global economy, opportunities for improvement

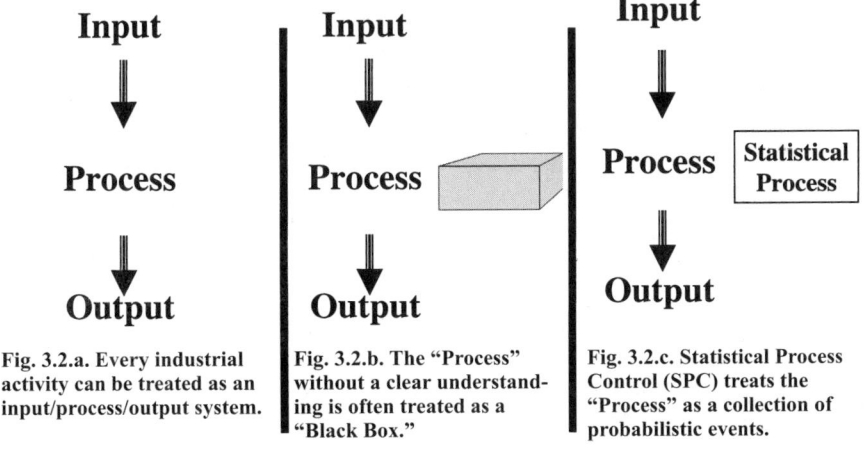

Fig. 3.2.a. Every industrial activity can be treated as an input/process/output system.

Fig. 3.2.b. The "Process" without a clear understanding is often treated as a "Black Box."

Fig. 3.2.c. Statistical Process Control (SPC) treats the "Process" as a collection of probabilistic events.

Figure 3.2 • Input/process/output system scenarios.

in financial performance can come from a few new or additional sources, such as lower labor cost on a worldwide basis, lower capital cost (due to national economic policies), global logistics, and information automation. These are resources available to the highest level managers of the enterprise. Those few who successfully utilize them to achieve improved financial performance are justifiably recognized and rewarded.[22] But for a larger cross-section of the population, the enterprise and its operation is nothing more than a black box. Hence, individuals participate in the jobs, which are more often a mere execution of tasks inside the black box.

The treatment of the process of the enterprise as a black box leaves behind untold consequences to the individuals or employees. In a larger sense, such a black box approach to the process is also the reason for gradual erosion of the long-term viability of any enterprise or industry. Superior financial performance alone is not a sufficient indicator of long-term strength and survivability. Instead, such performance needs to be intimately connected with the process that the enterprise is involved with in transforming chosen inputs to value or benefits (outputs) to its customers. There has been a general notion that an enterprise can be managed based on financial performance or other similar measures, without a clear and coherent understanding of the process engaged in by the industry or enterprise. This notion may have been appropriate in the past, but in the global economy it is a sure sign of long-term weakness for any enterprise or industry. The need to understand the process more than as a black box became evident just as the effects of globalization were being realized in the last 20 or 30 years.

In the absence of a clear definition, it is possible to treat the process as stochastic. In other words, variations in the process are recognized. But in the absence of a systematic and logical understanding, the variations are assumed to occur as random events. This is the definition of a stochastic process. Such treatment permits the process to be managed using statistical process control (SPC). (Figure 3.2.c.) SPC involves establishing a set of process measures and maintaining them within preestablished limits. If the process measures are held within the limits, the process is considered to be under control. A set of process measures can be established for each of the components of the enterprise. The entire enterprise can be managed by maintaining these process measures within the control limits. This approach is indeed valid when the process of the enterprise is nearly constant and is challenged by competitive pressures only in a limited and well-known environment. Enterprise management of this type has worked wonders in the past few decades. However, there are limitations to statistical process control in the global economy. These can be described through an analogy as follows.

Imagine a car being driven on the highway. The driver, John Pepke, knows the speed limit for the road. He has the option to maintain a lower speed limit, below which the car may become a danger to other vehicles on the road. To gain the advantage of shorter driving time (economic advantage), John can also choose an upper speed limit. Thus, the car is being driven between these two speed limits, periodically adjusting the components of the vehicle, such as brake, accelerator, etc., to stay within the control limits. In this case, the assigned job is the task of driving the specified car from point A to point B, on a path well defined and predetermined. If this car has been driven in this path many times before, the control limits are well established, and the corrective actions are well known. Under such a "task," statistical process control is an excellent tool to achieve the most reliable and predictable performance.

Now, John has been experiencing a gradual change in his job from one of merely driving from point A to point B. Instead, the enterprise or company requires him to transport objects from point A to point B. The objects could be people, physical goods, or information. Many of these objects are similar to those transported by John all along. For instance, John had previously transported people when necessary. He also has helped to move small packages along with the people. Routinely, John was also requested to drop off reports, messages or documents, or other information that needed to be hand delivered. If it needed to get there in a pinch, John could be relied upon to get it there. The company had once operated a fleet of vehicles, and employed many workers, such as John, engaged in similar jobs. As a cost cutting measure, many of these employees have been laid off. Also, to increase the capacity utilization, the fleet has been cut in half. Further, rules have been imposed to keep the fuel consumption cost under tight control. In addition, it has come to the attention of the employer that, if necessary, lower cost labor is available to replace John as the driver. The route that John used to follow has also changed. He has to take several paths instead of a pre-set route. The traffic patterns on these routes also change frequently.

All these changes in John Pepke's job are necessary to keep the enterprise competitive due to the pressures of globalization. The number of goods moved, fuel-cost, fleet capacity utilization etc., make excellent parameters for statistical process control. However, they do not adequately and appropriately represent the process that John Pepke is responsible for. Indeed, it will be necessary for John to define and describe the process which is his new job, and how it fits into the overall needs of the organization. The benefits of his process will be experienced by many of his customers, who can describe his process only from their perspective, which is limited at best. If John and his organization do not define the process, which is his new job, over a period of time the job will be reduced to a series of process measures or statistical parameters. The end result will be a series of arbitrary segmentations of the process into tasks and a possible loss of employment for John Pepke as the end result.

While it has advantages, SPC often brings with it an unwillingness or absence of focus to understand the process from a fundamental point of view. Consequently, SPC becomes progressively expensive. The excessive cost of traditional statistical process control methods, under global competitive pressures, is to some extent offset by the benefits of information automation. These benefits are being realized under many headings such as concurrent engineering, reengineering, etc.

It is well recognized that SPC serves a valuable and useful purpose, particularly when the process under consideration is stable and can be operated within well established limits. But the demands of globalization and the flexibility demanded by global processes requires an understanding of the process that goes beyond a purely statistical treatment.

There is a different, perhaps more appropriate, approach to describe the input/process/output sequence of any problem, job, or activity of an individual, organization, or enterprise. We shall call this the "System Approach."

Consider any enterprise in general. When asked to describe this enterprise as an input/process/output system, there will be hundreds of factors prescribed as inputs. The definition and description of these input factors will largely depend on the individual describing the enterprise. Indeed, extensive discussions on individual input factors and their role on influencing the function and destiny of the enterprise can be observed in numerous books on finance, management, engineering, science, human resource management, organizational studies, etc.

Just as there are hundreds of perceived inputs to the enterprise, there is an equally large number of outputs of an enterprise, again based on the perspective of the individual listing these outputs. Thus, any industrial activity would appear to be a multidimensional activity comprised of hundreds of inputs and outputs made possible through individuals, organizations, and their associated jobs, tasks, and functions. It is this perspective of any enterprise that renders its management as an "art," driven by changes and forces beyond the control of individuals, organizations, and the enterprise itself. This helplessness is compounded due to globalization as the numbers of input sources grow steadily, covering the entire globe. This helplessness is further compounded by the potential accessibility to markets around the world. Many real life experiences, as well as opinions, judgments, and frustrations arising from such a confounding scenario due to globalization have been outlined in Chapters 1 and 2. Many of these issues of globalization are at the organizational and enterprise level. However, many of them are also intrinsic and personal for every individual as they affect his/her job, career, personal life, and growth.

We can take a somewhat different approach. We can step back, far removed from the process pertinent to individual activity, organization, or enterprise, and look at it in its entirety. Then, distinct input groups emerge. These are:

- *Investment, Capital, and/or Other Fixed Assets.* In order for any industrial activity to exist and function, or even come to reality, certain resources associated with large sums of money are needed. Indeed, it is the access to this input category that fundamentally distinguishes the developed from developing nations. This input category may be observed in numerous forms. For example, equity, plant and equipment, machinery, information systems, research facilities, etc. In the traditional accounting parlance, these may be associated with fixed costs or assets of a company.
- *Distributed Resources.* These are the resources that are found distributed throughout the enterprise and often used or consumed during the process in small quantities. These include natural materials or their transformed alternatives. They also include tooling, consumables, or peripherals. Frequently, they are referred to as part of "Variable Cost." An enterprise takes these inputs and utilizes them or further transforms them into goods and services of value or use to society. Many nations became developed through their ability to successfully transform these inputs into more value added products and services. Many developing nations have these inputs, which are now becoming accessible for a larger range of worldwide enterprises, thanks to globalization. Conversely, many developing nations are in a position to further utilize their distributed resources thanks to the availability

of the previous input category (investments, capital, and/or other fixed assets) from the developed nations, due to globalization.

The skills of people as individuals as well as part of organizations—human resources—are an input factor available to an enterprise both as fixed investments and as distributed resources. Traditionally, these distributed aspects of human resources were thought of in a limited manner, such as physical labor to carry out assigned tasks. The global economy has transformed people and their skills into a distributed resource available on a worldwide basis in terms of physical labor, intellectual ability, and/or an ability to integrate and harness both along with other input categories. This transformation of human resources, as largely a distributed resource, is one of the fundamental and profound changes in the global economy.

- *Product or End-User Needs.* These are the customer's needs external to the enterprise and their requirements. Frequently, it will be mentioned that products are an output of the enterprise. Yet, every resource deployed by the enterprise, organization, or individual effort is intended to impact the product in some way. In reality, product or end-user needs serve as an input category on which other input factors are operated on by the enterprise.
- *Operational Environment.* These are the inputs that are unique and distinct for each enterprise, organization, or individual. For example, any two automotive manufacturers in the U.S. in theory have equal access to capital and other fixed assets, as well as the other two input resources—distributed resources and end-user needs—on a worldwide basis. Yet, the deployment of these three resources varies between these two companies. The factors that cause these variations in bringing together the three enterprise inputs—capital, distributed resources, and end-user needs—are what we will term the "operational factors."

In a similar fashion, one can look at any organization. Let us assume the same investments and facilities, capital or fixed assets, distributed resources, mission, or end-user needs. The deployment of these inputs will very from one organization to another. Indeed, these variations may be profoundly different for the same organization among different industries. This may be due to the skills of the employees, management style, etc. These are parameters or inputs within the organization. These inputs are all operational factors.

We can also look at an individual's job performance. Given the same resources, such as equipment/facilities, distributed resources, and the end-user needs, an individual brings to the job his/her personal skills, motivation and project or activity management skills that are inputs. When combined with the other inputs, these operational factors fundamentally alter the job performance of every employee.

Now, let us take a close look at the output of the process.

- *Technical Outputs.* These are output factors, readily obvious to those who are internal to or active participants in the process and its day-to-day details. These outputs can be described in terms and measures readily evident to those who actively participate in the tasks and functions of the enterprise. The technical outputs are often noted as responses to the question, "What is the process producing?"

    The traditional description of any enterprise is largely limited to technical outputs or internal performance measures of the enterprises. The overall benefit or output of the enterprise has frequently been looked at through limited financial measures such as the return on shareholder equity.

- *System Outputs.* These are the output factors readily discernible to those who benefit from the process and its existence. In a capitalistic society, these beneficiaries are easily identified as shareholders or investors in the input category identified as capital or fixed assets. The corresponding output is described as return on investment for the shareholders. However, every one of the input categories participates in the process of seeking benefits from the output of the process. The recent public discussions on stakeholder economy are largely a result of the need to focus on the output of the enterprise in terms of its employees and their benefits. There is another system output: The result or benefit of the process for other processes or systems with which it is integrally linked. These are generally identified as benefits to the supplier enterprises or industries, as well as the customer enterprises. Finally, the process by itself needs to be sustained, along with its physical as well as functional environment.

Thus, there are many participants in the process. Their contributions are recognized as belonging to one or more of the input categories. The number of participants in the process are relatively large. Hence, the number of investors in the process are far larger than those recognized as responsible for the financial inputs to the process. The system output of the process answers the question: "Why are we interested in the process?"

The system output is integrally linked to the technical output of the process. Yet, the two are not the same. They are linked to each other through definite causal relations, called "external causal relations," that are governed by factors outside of the process. These external causal relations may be the standard of living of the employees, price elasticity of the market, national economic policies, etc. These external causal relations are often influenced by factors beyond the internal control of the process. Hence, these external causal relations are also beyond the direct influence or control of organizations or individuals in the enterprise. Yet, clarity and focus on such external causal relations is essential in our understanding and management of the enterprise as a system. In the global economy, the external causal relationships are frequently influenced by national economic policies, which in turn are influenced by the society and its political process.

In addition to the input and output system components already described, every process involves certain well-defined microscopic process interactions. In engineering systems, these are frequently referred to as "transfer functions." In physical processes, these are described as the "phenomena." In chemical processes, these are described as the "reactions." In human relationships, these are described as "interpersonal dynamics." In the case of an enterprise, these microscopic interactions may be described as "core competence." We shall discuss the core competence in detail in the latter part of this section.

No matter how they are characterized, each process has associated with it certain microscopic process interactions, whose manifestations are quantified by the macroscopic process variables. Conversely, the macroscopic process variables are the descriptors of the microscopic process interactions. The "internal causal relations" define the linkage between the process interactions and their measurements. Causal relations may be laws of science, engineering principles, internal dynamics of an enterprise, etc., depending on the process involved.

Hence, it is possible to define any industrial activity as an input/output transformation process with defined internal causal relations and equally well-defined external causal relations. The more complete the description of the system, the more comprehensive our understanding of the enterprise. In the era of globalization, as jobs and enterprises evolve from executing tasks to solving problems, description of the activity as a system becomes the essential and fundamental prerequisite. The more comprehensive the description of the system, the more comprehensive the definition of the problem. It is worth remembering the adage that "defining the problem is the better half of the solution."

This approach to industrial activities as input/process/output system is illustrated in Figure 3.3.

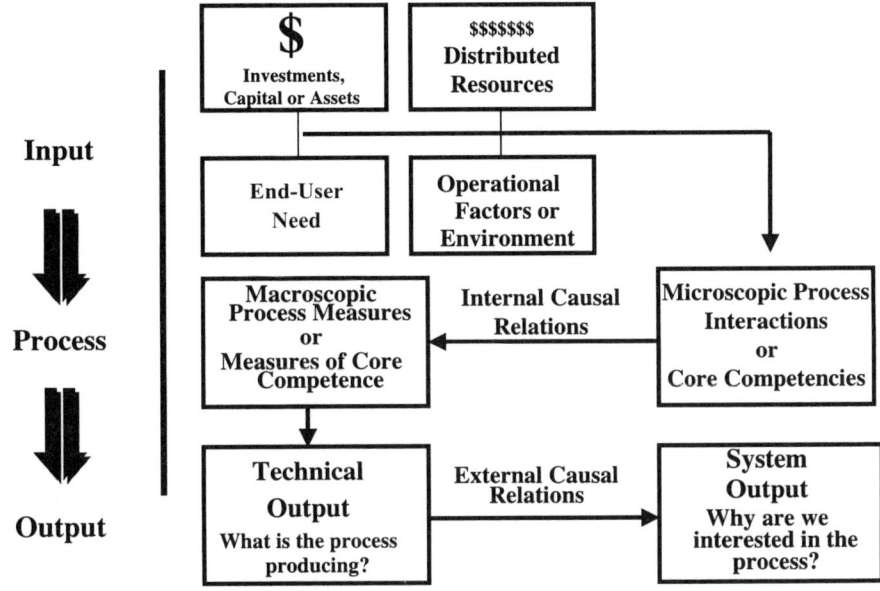

Figure 3.3 • The System Approach for industrial processes.

Such a System Approach to problem definition is not a mere hypothetical or theoretical exercise. Instead, such an approach provides a rational means for handling a wide range of issues associated with globalization. In the past, such systems did exist and individuals executed tasks within the system. It was left to the organization and its managers to integrate the tasks into a system. Engineering activities were always handled as a project. "Project management" is a common term used to define the system and the execution of the transformation process to achieve the desired end-results. Engineering systems and their control are often based on definitions of transfer function (internal causal relation) and their manipulation.

As the jobs are transformed from task execution to problem resolution, the need for the System Approach is increasingly evident. Enterprises need to define their core competence, which is the essential element of their competitive advantage. Traditionally, such core competence of the enterprise was deployed into practice by the organizations in the enterprise,

64 • The System Approach

each with their own set of core competencies. Individuals within the organization participated in the process and succeeded through their individual competencies. These sets of competencies (enterprise, organization, and individual) were often available in a distributed fashion. They were considered as competitive advantages. The enterprise that harnessed the best collection of these independent competencies was most successful in the industry. Nevertheless, due to globalization, the best collection of these competencies is no longer sufficient. Instead, a systematic integration of an optimum combination of these competencies in every level, individual, organization, and the enterprise, is very much needed.

The enterprise, as a transformation engine with core competencies at every level, is shown in Figure 3.4. The core competence of the enterprise is the transfer function, which transforms the inputs into outputs. In the era of globalization, the core competence of an enterprise can be defined as technol-

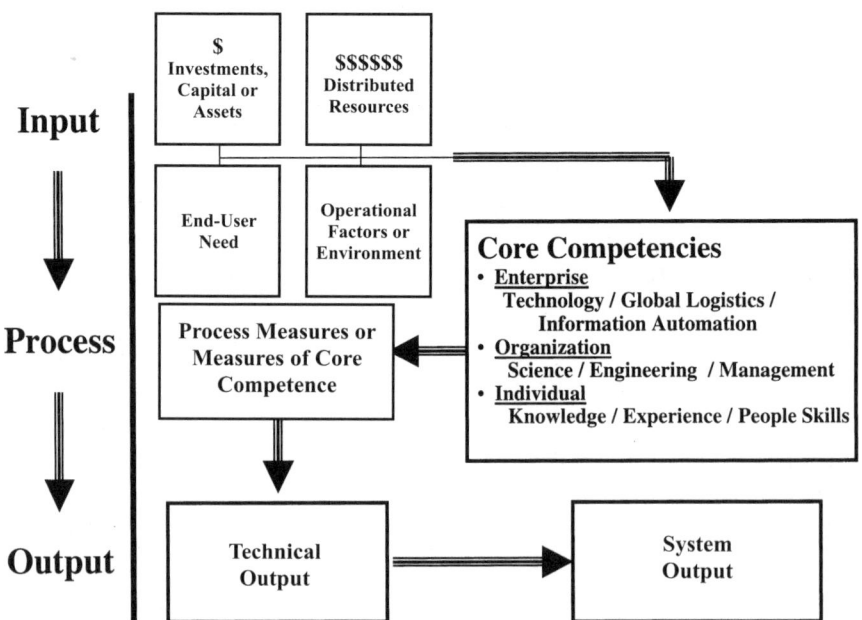

Figure 3.4 • System Approach. Synergistic deployment of core competencies at every level: enterprise, organization and individual. The "input/process/output" system in each case remains identical.

ogy, information automation, and global logistics. While it was possible to maintain the competitive advantage with strength in one of these three core competencies, globalization requires a simultaneous competence in all three areas.

We have expressed the enterprise as a system, but it does not function in isolation. Its success largely depends on the effectiveness of its organizations and the individuals in the organization. The organization-wide competence governing the enterprise can be defined as Science, Engineering, and Management. It was possible in the past to maintain the competitive advantage through strength in one or more of these areas. Globalization requires a simultaneous competence of any organization in all three areas.

The individual competencies required for success in any organization are knowledge, experience, and people skills. While it was once possible to achieve success through one of these three areas, success in today's globalized economy requires individuals to be competent in all three areas simultaneously.

The core competencies for the organization include the core competencies of the individuals in the organization. The enterprise, in turn, requires the competencies of its organization

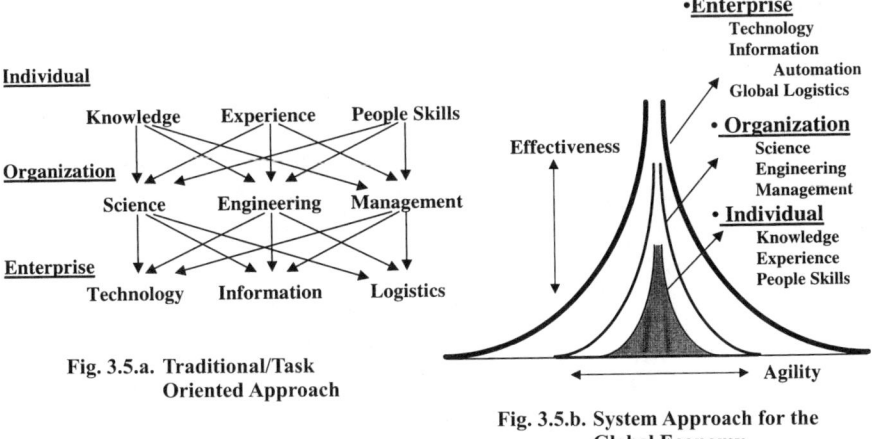

Figure 3.5 • *The System Approach. Integrated deployment of core competencies of the enterprise, organization and individuals.*

and the employees in each organization. This interdependence between the enterprise/organization/individual is shown in Figure 3.5.

None of the core competencies, outlined in Figures 3.4 or 3.5, is definable in specific quantitative terms, nor can physical objects represent any of them. These are the intangibles of any enterprise. These are also the transfer functions, which transform the inputs into outputs. Manipulating these core competencies (microscopic interactions) would appear to be the heart and soul of every enterprise, organization, or individual. These core competencies or microscopic interactions do not recognize or understand geographic barriers. Therein lies the genesis of globalization.

Measures of the competence of the enterprise, organization, or individual are many and varied. Yet, they must truly reflect or represent the core competencies identified. Otherwise, the performance of the enterprise, organization, or the individual may be measured and monitored precisely, but the internal causal relations may not be adequately captured or understood.

Small changes in the internal causal relations can lead to quantum changes in the output of the system. This is well known by scientists and engineers. Surprisingly, it is also true for every industrial activity at any level, from an individual worker to the enterprise or the industry.

The internal causal relations of the process are the cause and effect relationships between the process (microscopic interactions) and their measurements. These internal causal relations can be managed by strategically changing the input variables. If one or a few inputs are changed at a time, the change in output is often incremental in nature. Frequently, such small changes in output may not be perceived or measurable due to random variations in other input variables and their impact on the output. This may be frequently described as the "noise" in the output measures. On the other hand, strategic and simultaneous change of several inputs, from all of the input categories with a clear understanding of modulating specific few internal causal relations, often leads to quantum changes in the output of the system. Remember, quantum improvements in output are one of the requirements for success in a global economy.

To summarize, the System Approach involves the following:
- Industrial activity is described in terms of "Input/Process/Output" system.
- The input variables to the "process" can be broadly grouped under four categories:
  1) Investments, capital or assets,
  2) Distributed resources,
  3) End-user needs,
  4) Operational factors.
- Control of one input variable at a time leads to incremental changes in the output (better mousetrap). These improvements are often masked by unknown variations in other input variables.
- The output of the process can be delineated between Technical Outputs—What is the process producing? System Outputs—Why are we interested in the "process?"
- Establish the external causal relationships governing the process. These relations are the link between the technical and the system outputs of the process. These external causal relations also establish the strategic needs of the stakeholders of the process and how they are to be met through the output factors familiar to those intimately involved in the process.
- The objective in the global economy is to achieve large scale or quantum changes in the system outputs (different mousetrap).
- The process is a transformation engine composed of a few core competencies at every level.
  1) Enterprise—Technology, Global Logistics, Information Automation
  2) Organizational—Science, Engineering, Management
  3) Individual Level—Knowledge, Experience, People Skills.
- Establish the internal causal relationships governing the

problem. These relations link the core competencies (microscopic interactions) with the macroscopic process measures.
- Small changes in the internal causal relations can lead to quantum changes in the output.
- Simultaneous strategic changes in a few selected input variables from each of the four input groups to change the internal causal relationships governing the system often leads to quantum improvements in the output of the process (different mousetrap).
- The System Approach focuses on solving the problem by looking at the input/process/output system as a whole and not on executing a task, which is a partial representation of the system.
- Thus, the System Approach permits an individual to span over a wide range of tasks with a focus on problem-solving. This promotes agility and effectiveness simultaneously.
- The internal causal relationships governing the system
  1) Creates the common language within the enterprise or organization.
  2) Creates the common language between several enterprises, which are all collective participants in the process.
  3) Establishes the basis of the enterprise, organization, or individual and its focus area.
  4) Determines the vectors for developments.
  5) Establishes a rational basis for expansion, acquisition and/or diversification at the enterprise, organization, or individual level.
- The engineering activities are integrated within the enterprise, organization, or individual job functions through the internal and external causal relationships, which
  1) Facilitates inter-industry collaboration.
  2) Creates synergy within the functions of the company.
  3) Facilitates leveraging of core competencies at every level.

- The core competencies that represent the microscopic process interaction at each level—enterprise, organization, and individual—create a seamless alignment of everyone involved in the process. This leads to the viewpoints of, "Management is everybody's business," and interdisciplinary thought process precedes and facilitates interdisciplinary teamwork.
- This in turn enhances overall productivity, which permeates in every aspect of the enterprise.

In the following chapters, we will further elaborate on the System Approach, and its use from enterprise level considerations to the individual worker.

Chapter 4

The Enterprise and the System Approach

The consequence of globalization of the economy is the challenge to be the best in every activity, with the whole world as the playing field as well as the source of competition. This is true for individuals, organizations, or enterprises. This need for transformation was described in detail in the previous chapters. A well-established practice used to judge whether we meet this challenge is to seek a set of comparative measures called "benchmarks" and quantification based on such benchmarks. This is an expensive and tedious approach, as well as arbitrary at best. Benchmarks are based on what has already been achieved. They provide measures of what has been, rather than provide directions for what could be. When the marketplace is global, the competition is also global. In this scenario, traditional means of benchmarking may not be sufficient.

Another way to maintain competitive advantage is to seek

quantum or substantial improvements in the performance or productivity of every activity. In the global economy, the level of improvement in productivity expected is substantially larger than previously conceived possible. This is true for individuals, organizations, or the enterprise taken as a whole.

If we agree to improve the productivity of every activity, in a quantum manner, the question arises as to how one defines the "activity?" In the traditional approach, an individual could, for example, seek productivity improvement through improved management of their personal time, communication effectiveness, on-time completion of selected tasks or projects or commitments, etc. Similarly, an organization could set productivity goals in terms of reduced rejections, on-time delivery, time bringing new product to market, meeting budgets, achievement of sales targets, etc. At the enterprise level, the productivity measures typically used are often financial in nature, such as return on investment (ROI), return on net asset (RONA), sales per employee, profit per employee, etc. In all these traditional descriptions, the "activity" is defined in disconnected and arbitrary terms, frequently in terms of a myriad of tasks carried out by individuals, organizations, or enterprises. Such task descriptions are then linked in a painstaking manner. A collection of tasks leads to an organization and an enterprise in that order. The individual's job is often described in terms of tasks, such as design, planning, purchasing, sales, assembly, supervision, customer service, accounting, administration, management, etc. The functions of organization are described in terms of a collection of tasks such as research, manufacturing, marketing, sales, management, etc. Then constant improvements in specific measures of these individual tasks or activities are sought either against predetermined benchmarks or through continuous improvements.

As a result of globalization, the fundamental change in the nature of employment is the transition from task oriented job assignment to problem resolution oriented job functions. This transition was described in earlier chapters. Many of the job functions of the past, which were largely tasks of information collection, processing, and dissemination, are now largely being eliminated through means of "information automation." Similarly, there is an enormous increase in the ability to gather, transfer, and manage complex sets of information as well as physical goods and other resources. Such increased ability has been achieved through the means of information processing technology, communication technology, and transportation technology. This has enabled the enterprises to utilize worldwide resources in the execution of tasks at every level, from conceptual thinking, to engineering, to manufacturing, to management. We call this "global logistics." As much as inputs or resources for an enterprise have been multiplied (utilizing multiple resources from anywhere in the world), so has there been a multiplication in the distribution and sales outlets for products or outputs of an enterprise for a wide range of markets, accessible worldwide. This has transformed every industrial activity from a collection of tasks to a "system" involving multiple sources of inputs and multiple channels for the outputs. This transition in industrial activity from the traditional to global economy has been illustrated in Figure 2.4. Thus, every industrial activity may be viewed as a "system," that transforms the inputs to outputs through the "process." In a traditional economy, the process could rely on one or a few specific core competencies of individuals, organizations, or enterprises. In the global economy, the process becomes a means for effective and simultaneous deployment of few core competencies, not as scattered or isolated individual competencies. For success, they have to be deployed in an integrated and simultaneous set of core competencies. This description of an industrial enterprise, with multiple inputs from anywhere in the world, and a transformation process simultaneously driven by technology, information automation and global logistics, leading to outputs anywhere in the world, is described in Figure 2.5.

Thus, every job of an individual, organization, and the enterprise may be described as an input/process/output system. In the global economy, every job at every level of the organization becomes a "system," through the integration of multiple tasks. Today, benchmarks refer to the performance measurement of individual tasks. In a global economy, benchmarks have to become measures of the system output. Similarly, benchmarked productivity refers to gains in an individual's tasks or functions. In the global economy, productivity measures will refer to the overall gain of the input/process/output system. The objective in the global economy, for every job function, will be to achieve quantum improvements in the productivity of the "process."

Now let's discuss the definition of the "system" for an enterprise, and its identification through its components. A generic model for the System Approach has been outlined as noted in Figure 3.3. Its applicability for industrial processes has been illustrated in Figure 3.4. Extensive discussion and definition of every industrial activity and its associated "system" is, of course, beyond the scope of this book. However, we shall use two extreme cases, as follows. The first case will describe an enterprise in generic terms and how it can be configured as an input/process/output system. This System Approach to the enterprise is dealt with in this chapter. The second case will involve any industrial activity described as a "unit process" and its configuration as a system. These descriptions of the job functions of the individual and organization as a "system" will be discussed in the next chapter. The chapter that follows will describe the application of the System Approach for enterprise management, product/process development, engineering jobs within an enterprise, and also for education and career development.

Every enterprise may be thought of as a system with a large number of inputs. The interaction of these inputs—or the process—culminates in certain outputs. This simple description of the overall enterprise as a system is shown in Figure 4.1. Traditionally, it has been possible to manipulate one or a few of these input factors at a time to achieve variations in output of significant value to the enterprise. In the global economy, this focus on individual factors is being replaced by a need

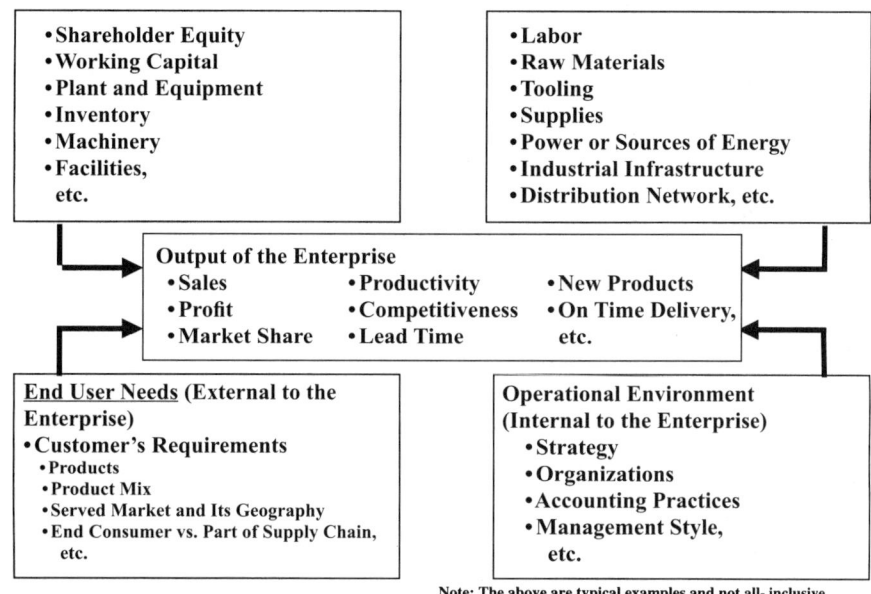

Figure 4.1 • Typical input and output variables to an enterprise.

to focus on groups of factors or the individual input categories. All the input factors shown in Figure 4.1 can be classified among one of the four input categories shown in Figure 4.2. Each of the input groupings in Figure 4.2 contains within itself a large number of individual factors. Traditional economy relied on limited movement and use of resources across geographies. In the global economy, every one of these input factors among these four input categories is a candidate for movement or accessibility across the globe.

Capital as an input category can now be moved from one enterprise to another, independent of geographic limitations. Moving capital and other sources of investments across various countries is a common occurrence today. The existence and success of global mutual funds is a case in point. The acquisition and merger of companies across continents is another example of the mobility of capital on a global basis. Utilizing the results of human effort across geographies was once restricted to the use of physical labor or other work per-

76 • The System Approach

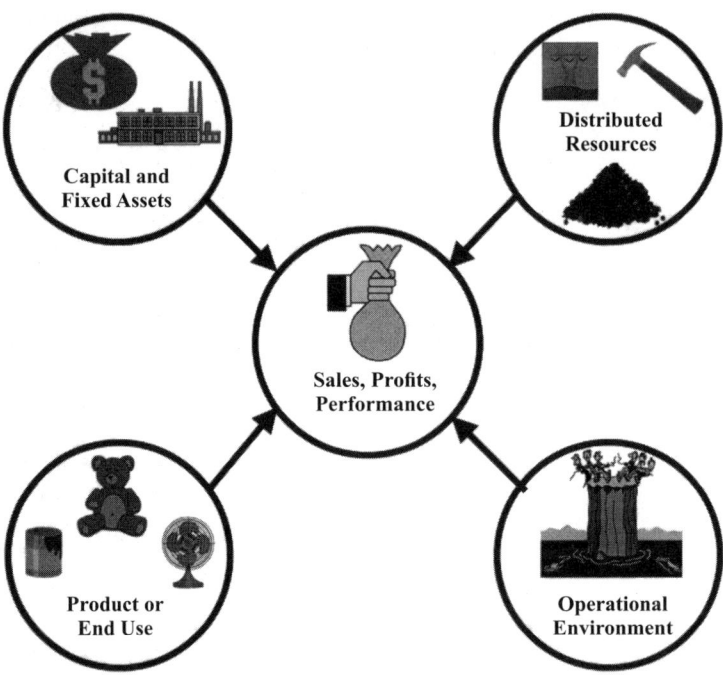

Figure 4.2 • Industrial enterprise viewed as an input/output system.

formed by a blue-collar work force. Now human resources of every kind—from plant labor to engineering to management—are utilized across once unimaginable geography as a result of globalization. The use of raw materials and similar resources from anywhere in the world is nothing new to any industrialist. Thanks to the advent of "global logistics," the nature and extent of the use of worldwide raw material and manpower resources are changing dramatically. Here, the "distributed resources" are not basic or unprocessed raw materials such as ores and minerals. Instead, this input category represents the physical, consumable resources of any kind pertaining to an enterprise. Thus ores, minerals, blank stock, semi-finished components, finished components, sub-assemblies, are all part of the input category. All of these are now described as "distributed resources" to the enterprise, at different levels.

Now, let's take a close look at the outputs of the enterprise.

These outputs can be described in individual terms as listed in Figure 4.1. Alternatively, they can be classified into two groups, as shown in Figure 4.3.

The output of an enterprise can be divided in two categories: "technical" output or those output measures which are readily understood by those intimately involved in the process, and "system" output which describes the value or benefit of the "process" for the intended "customer"—the ultimate beneficiary of the "process." The difference between the system outputs and technical outputs can be illustrated as shown in Figure 4.3. Every industrial activity can be described through this simple statement: "We make money when we make and sell the products that the customers use and want." This process, is shown as an endless cycle in Figure 4.3. It shows a right half (technical output) and left half (system output). The

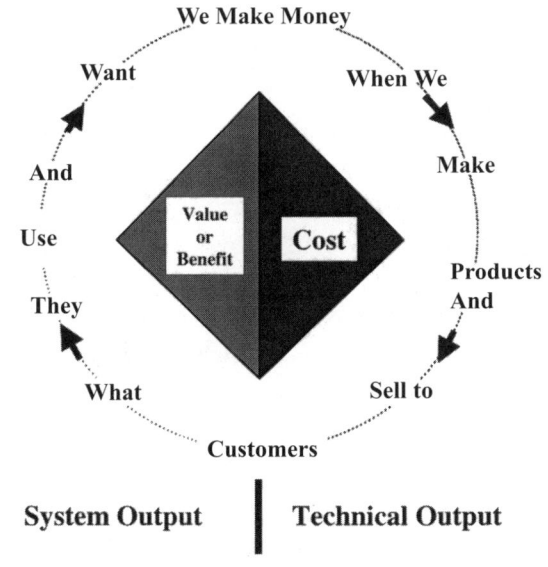

Use: End-User Requirements today.
Want: End-User Requirements for tomorrow.

Figure 4.3 • The outputs of any industrial activity may be classified in two groups: technical and system outputs.

right half consists of activities well known inside the enterprise, including the products, their design, manufacture, distribution, and sales to customers. These are the technical outputs of the enterprise. They are also part of the cost or operation of the enterprise. However, these outputs do not transform into value or benefits unless customers find that the products meet their needs and they want to use the products. At the end of the day, satisfying these "needs" and "wants" of the customer that occur external to the enterprise is the real or final output of the "system." "Needs" are the requirements of the customer today. "Wants" are the requirements of the customer tomorrow. Together they make up the system output. In simplest terms, the closer the technical output of the enterprise is linked to the customer's needs and wants, the more successful the enterprise.

The differences between the "technical output" and the "system output" may not be readily apparent at first sight. These two outputs are linked by economic factors as well as value/benefit relationships. The technical output of a process may be the same anywhere in the world, but the resultant system output could vary depending on geographic, economic, cultural, and political factors. The need to recognize and understand the relationships between the technical and the system output is of growing importance in the global economy.

As the enterprise becomes more of a part of the global economy—which we have already discussed as inevitable—the individuals in the enterprise can no longer assume these external causal relations as a constant or a given. Thus, management of an enterprise solely through technical outputs and their optimization, which was acceptable in a localized economy, is no longer valid in the global economy.

The enterprise as a "system" will be truly successful only when every one of the contributors to the "inputs" gains benefits or value through the outputs of the system. This is a simple fact: No one participates in any industrial activity through altruistic motives. Hence, a true and complete management of the system requires consideration of the system output for all stakeholders (i.e., every constituent who participates through one or more of the four input groups). Consideration of "end-user needs and wants" addresses benefits for only one of the four input groups. In many enterprises, while end-user needs and wants are emphasized, the true expectation of the enterprise managers is more often than not to increase the "shareholder value."

In the traditional economy, individual enterprises and their activities were restricted to a few nations with similar economic styles. While the enterprise focused on partial system outputs, the nations and their economic planners focused on the rest of the system output. This collective but segmented effort was sufficient to meet the needs of all stakeholders of any enterprise. Such isolated focus on parts of the system outputs may no longer be adequate or satisfactory in the global economy.

The chief executive of an enterprise who argues for maximizing shareholder return as his/her only goal offers only a limited view of the system output. Perhaps such partial consideration of the system output was valid at an earlier time, but it is not valid in the global economy. When a purchasing agent wishes to reduce the cost of the raw material inputs, to maximize performance efficiency for his/her organization by using the lowest cost resources from anywhere in the world, it is a valid and desirable objective. Such an objective is perfectly valid and very much desirable for the success of his/her enterprise. However, such performance of the purchasing agent is merely an execution of the task to achieve a technical output, without regard for many system output factors, such as long term success and viability of supplier enterprises, as well as the long term success and viability of his/her own enterprise and its environment.

When the enterprise is viewed as a system, the ultimate output of every employee, from the chief executive to the lowest level employee, is the same. This is shown as the "system output" in Figure 4.4. Without a common focus, the enterprise will function as a disconnected entity with multiples of internal output measures (identified as "technical output" in Figure 4.4). The organizations and procedures required to support such conflicting objectives will be complex indeed. Such complexities may be non-sustainable and can ultimately become a competitive disadvantage in the global economy.

The system output is not an isolated occurrence independent of the technical output. Indeed, there is a close causal relationship between the two. Frequently these relationships are governed by factors external to the enterprise. In the traditional economy, these are identified as market dynamics, price elasticity, consumer behavior, etc. In a global economy, enterprises work across many preferred economic styles (depending on the politics and cultural practices of various nations). Hence, the number of external causal relationships is much larger than would be considered necessary in traditional practices. In addition, an understanding of these external causal relationships was expected only from corporate managers as

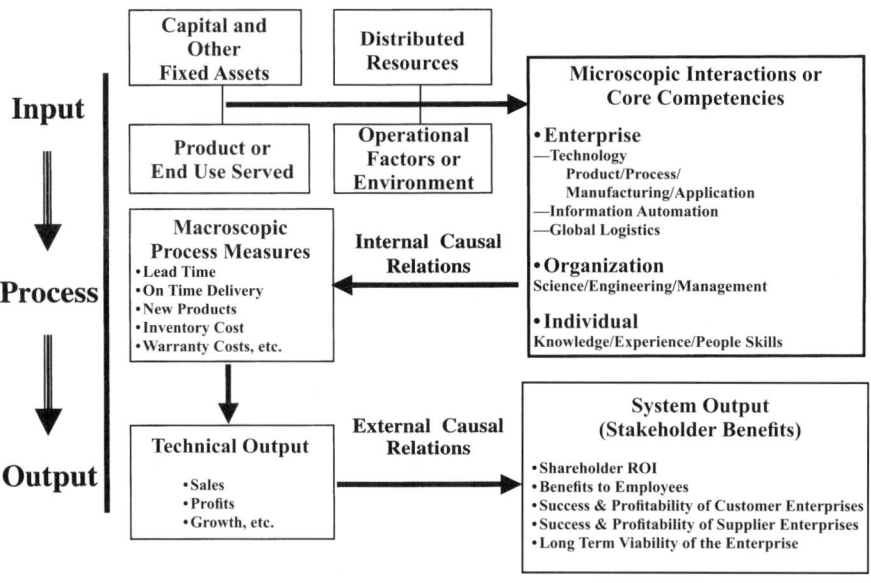

Figure 4.4 • The enterprise viewed as an "input/process/output" system.

part of their "strategic planning." However, in the global economy, understanding and assimilating these external causal relations is required at every level of the enterprise.

Thus far, we have described the inputs and outputs of the enterprise viewed as a system. The transformation between the inputs and the outputs is the "process" of the enterprise. The "process" is frequently recognized through a set of measures of the process. We shall call these the "macroscopic variables." These are measurements or quantifications of the process and its characteristics. Typical examples of these "macroscopic process variables" are shown in Figure 4.4. Traditionally, individuals and organizations utilize these process measures as the output of their individual job or the output of their organization. Such an approach was appropriate and acceptable when the job was limited to performing individual tasks. But, when the job function is transformed into one of "problem resolution," one's focus must be concentrated on the outputs of the system. Continued reliance on macroscopic process measures, as the output of the enterprise and its organizations, is a sure sign for failure for the following reasons:

- A problem resolution oriented job, assignment, or organization is expected to deliver the results or outputs of significance to the entire system. Macroscopic process measures by themselves do not represent the system output. Instead, they are more a measure of the core competence or inner workings of the enterprise.
- Many of the macroscopic process measures and their tracking can be accomplished through means of information automation. An organization focused on measurement or management of the macroscopic process measures will be gradually diminished, if not eliminated, through tools of "information automation" and "global logistics."
- As the expectations of the output of the system shift, due to changes in external causal relations, the organization or individuals have to respond with different techni-

cal outputs. Confusing macroscopic process measures with the output hinders or limits flexibility and the required rapid competitive response. In another words, agility and flexibility are required in the technical output of the system, consistent with changes in external causal relations as they occur. However, such agility is difficult to accomplish when the focus of the output is limited to macroscopic process variables.
- Relating the inputs to the outputs is part of the management of the system. Too frequently, individuals such as the engineers trained in specialized areas limit their focus on measurement and monitoring of the physical process variables. As we discussed earlier, such task oriented job functions do not exist or are vanishing rapidly in a global economy.

Referring again to Figure 4.4, there are certain core competencies that are essential to the transformation "process" of the enterprise. We have discussed core competencies and their role in some detail in Chapter 3, where it was pointed out that, in the past, excellence in one of the core competencies, or an arbitrary combination of them, was sufficient to achieve success. Indeed this may be true even today for some individuals and small companies. But as the organization becomes larger and as the enterprise becomes more integrated with the global economy, such arbitrary selection among these core competencies will cease to be adequate. Indeed, a strategic, synergistic, and systematic integration of competencies of individuals, organizations, and the enterprise as a whole is the new paradigm.

Earlier, we discussed core competence of a globalized enterprise in terms of technology, information automation, and global logistics. An enterprise may consist of several organizations, each specializing in certain technology. The information automation and global logistics could be the same or shared across the various organizations.

Too often, it is the "technology" of the enterprise, as a core competence, which is the least understood. Yet, like the spinal column, it is the technology that provides the stability and functional capability for an enterprise. In the absence of clear and comprehensive understanding of the relevant technology as its core competence, enterprises are often managed purely in terms of financial measures. As we stated earlier, finance or capital is one of the key input groupings. Also, finance or return on investor's equity is a key system output. In this respect the role of finance at these extremes (input and output) of the system is apparent. Yet, the transformation process of the enterprise is affected by technology as a core competence. While financial factors or measures enable the effectiveness of core competence, they by themselves are not the core competencies. This should be clearly understood and articulated effectively by technologists in an enterprise. Before such advocacy can occur, the technologists must themselves be clear of what is it that they are dealing with in terms of "technology."

In the age of excessive opportunities for measurement and manipulation of information, technology as the representation of the physical phenomena is too often forgotten. Understanding the physical phenomena is frequently the role of the scientists. As the engineers focus on measurement and management of the technology through countless parameters, there is little time or interest to understand the underlying phenomena. When engineers abrogate the understanding of the phenomena, they become more like technicians managing parameters than engineers managing the processes. When scientists do not articulate the phenomena in terms of macroscopic process measures relevant for an enterprise, the role of technology is superseded by other easily measurable parameters. Thus, the "science" base of an organization is substituted by empirical efforts. There is no need to state the obvious, that management is a key component of any process. This is true for any organization. Thus, science, engineering, and management are the three core competencies of any organization. An enterprise consists of many organizations each with its distinct set of core competencies in science, engineering, and management. All three of these core competencies are the channels through which the enterprise level core competencies of technology, information automation, and global logistics are deployed.

Now let us look at the "technology" of an enterprise in some detail. Technology of any enterprise may be divided into four categories (see Table 4.1).

Product Technology. This is the science, engineering, and management associated with the "product" sold by the enterprise, in exchange for revenue. The "product" may be physical units or any other unit of value to the customer or end-user.

Process Technology. Process is the method or physical transformation necessary in achieving the "product." The "process" technology involves effective deployment of science, engineering, and management in the use of "process" to achieve the "product".

Manufacturing Technology. This is the implementation or repetitive use of the "processes" to achieve the "products" in desired quantity, place, and time. Thus, manufacturing technology by its very nature involves extensive use of information

---

Table 4.1
Technology of an enterprise can be grouped into four categories.

1. **Product Technology**
   The knowledge or know-how to configure the "mouse trap" for an intended function. Product is the object, or any other unit of value, which is exchanged for the revenue of an enterprise.

2. **Process Technology**
   The knowledge or know-how to reduce the configured "mouse trap" into a physical reality.

3. **Manufacturing Technology**
   The knowledge or know-how required for the repetitive uses of the process to achieve the product in the desired quantity, place and time.

4. **Application Technology**
   The knowledge or know-how that links all technology functions of an enterprise with the "needs" and "wants" to be satisfied for the end customer, when using the "mouse trap."

and logistics in addition to the product and process technologies. In the global economy, manufacturing as a technology has made enormous gains through appropriate deployment of information automation and global logistics. While these improvements will continue, the next wave of improvements in manufacturing technology will be aided by advancements in product and process technologies. The terms "quality" and "cost" are associated with manufacturing. In reality, these are the macroscopic measures of the core competencies in product, process, and manufacturing technologies.

Application Technology. This is the science, engineering, and management as they relate to the application or use of the "products" of the enterprise by its end customers.

Of the four categories, the first three—the product, the process, and the manufacturing technologies—are studied in detail in a number of publications. We shall now discuss the "Application Technology" in some detail.

Figure 4.5 describes application technology in a schematic manner. Unlike the "product" or "process" technology, the "application" technology is not easily defined. Yet, it is gov-

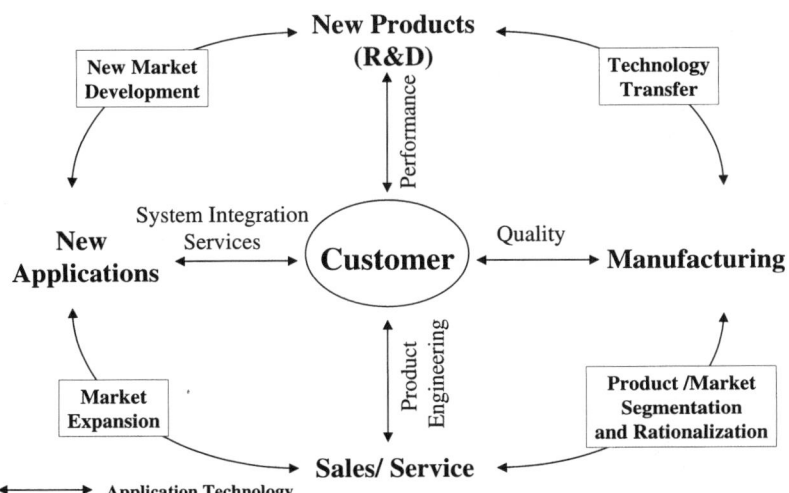

Figure 4.5 • *Many functions of critical importance to any enterprise are linked to the end-user's "needs" and "wants" through the application technology.*

erned by scientific principles, engineering practices, and management rigors very similar to other technologies. Application technology helps an enterprise develop a customer-centered viewpoint, which is very much needed and yet very difficult to achieve in the day-to-day operation of an enterprise. The System Approach facilitates this process since evaluation of technology, as a core competence in a system-oriented enterprise, invariably requires evaluation of the competence in application technology.

Application technology pertains to the understanding of the "performance" of the product to meet customer requirements. Application technology, in this respect, will be noted in all the testing laboratories of an enterprise. Too frequently, these testing laboratories are tucked away at the back of many research and development or manufacturing facilities. Lack of clear and comprehensive understanding of product performance in terms of customer needs leads to poor quality of testing, frequently in terms of arbitrary engineering parameters. Conversely, the competence to represent the customer performance expectations through controlled experimental equipment and procedures (performance testing) facilitates accelerated product development, allows for a reduction in time to market, and provides greater access to customer intimacy.

Application technology also refers to the assessment of quality in terms of performance consistency of the product as seen from the end customer's point of view. "Quality" in this regard is not merely the product attributes as measurable parameters or specifications. Instead, specifications for quality standards are manifestations in terms of product function and reliability in the eyes of the customer. Without such an understanding of the phenomena, quality is too frequently translated into engineering parameters. When communication permeates through parameters, without understanding of the underlying phenomena, the "quality" becomes more and more a statistical parameter.

Sales/service, as viewed from the technology considerations

and from the customer's perspective, is the engineering or repeated application of the product to meet the customer's functional needs. Thus, application-engineering activities of the sales/service function are governed by an understanding of the product in terms of its performance and functional quality in the customer's environment. New applications or novel solutions emerge, as the "product" is integrated with the equipment used by the customer in their applications. This is frequently referred to as "system integration." The customer is directly involved in all of these aspects of application technology. In addition, there are many internal interactions such as product/process technology transfer, product rationalization, market expansion, and new/emerging market development, where application technology plays a crucial role. Thus, application technology may be thought of as the nerve system inside the enterprise or in the interactions between related enterprises. Every one of these interfaces has measurable impact on the end customer.

It is clear from the above that in addition to the three categories of technologies—product, process, and manufacturing—there is a fourth component of technology called application technology. This technology integrally links various functions within the enterprise. It also links the customer closely to the various internal organizations of the enterprise, as well as with associated industries (Figure 4.6.). In many respects, application technology provides a critical linkage between all the technological core competencies of an enterprise as shown in Figure 4.7.

In the age of globalization, product and process technology can be acquired or developed anywhere in the world. Traditionally, R&D has been thought of as the source for all novel ideas for the enterprise. Indeed, in the global economy R&D becomes more of an identifier of novel ideas from anywhere in the world, and the integrator of these ideas into the product or process technologies of the enterprise. Similarly, manufacturing technology can be developed and deployed utilizing the most prudent resources available anywhere in the

88 • The System Approach

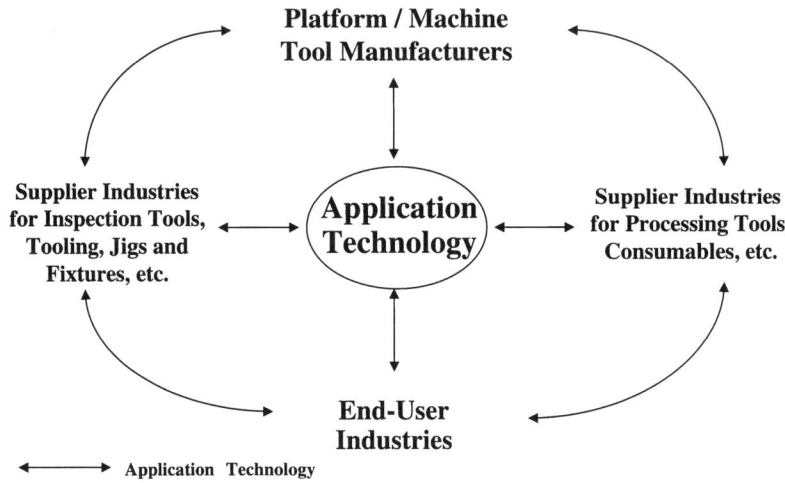

Figure 4.6 • Application technology provides the common language between related industries in any industrial activity.

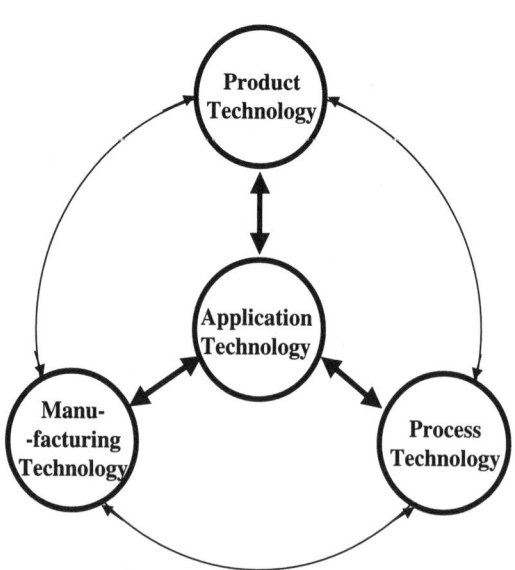

Figure 4.7 • Application technology provides the linkage between all technology based core competencies of an enterprise.

world. Then, it is application technology that integrally links the enterprise to its internal functions as well as to its end customers. Hence, deployment of application technology as a core competence is an essential element of success and differentiation in the context of globalization. Such development of application technology through individual or unit manufacturing processes will be discussed later in this book.

The core competencies provide a rational alternative for providing measures of the process. These measures, called "macroscopic measures," should be limited in number. They can reflect the measures of the core competencies individually, or in any desired combination. These process measures are linked to the core competencies through "internal causal relationships." In many respects, the choice of macroscopic process measures reflects the understanding of the "process" engaged in by the enterprise and the core competencies deployed by the enterprise. These internal causal relationships also reflect every one of the core competencies at the enterprise, organization, and individual level, and their deployment through the interaction of all the four input categories.

Having defined the enterprise system and its components now allows us to look for a means to achieve quantum improvements in the output of the system. The system outputs are clearly delineated in terms of five stakeholders of the enterprise—the investors, the employees, the supplier industries, the end-user industries, and the enterprise itself.

- First, all the system outputs must be clearly identified for everyone involved with the enterprise. It must also be explicit that quantum improvements will be sought in all of the system outputs or in a chosen few. The selection, magnitude, and nature of improvements desired in the system output, and desired balance among the system outputs indeed becomes the "vision" of the enterprise. The vision is evident and readily obvious to those who are inside the enterprise, as well as to those who are connected with and are external to the enterprise. The specified changes desired in the system output permits their translation in terms of technical outputs of significance or relevance to those inside the enterprise.

This approach is fundamentally different from the current practice in most enterprises, where the technical outputs are the stated goals of the company. Their translation to system output is considered only in terms of shareholder return on investment. All other system outputs are assumed to happen by chance or as undirected consequences.

This clarification of the vision of the enterprise through the system output by itself has enormous consequences. Every individual, organization, and the enterprise as a whole is now committed to the same common goal. The beneficiaries of the system output are every constituent involved in the system—the investors, the employees, the supplier industries, as well as customer industries and the enterprise itself. The expectation of relative benefit among these constituents is clarified and readily understood. This is not an altruistic statement. Instead, it is a logical outcome when the enterprise is viewed as a whole.

- Quantum changes in the system output are made possible through strategic changes in the core competencies. The core competencies are identified as:
    Enterprise: Technology, information automation, and global logistics.
    Organization: Science, engineering, and management.
    Individual: Knowledge, experience, and people skills.

At every level, the core competence is deployed not as an isolated or individual effort. Instead, it is deployed as a cluster in coherence with the cluster of core competencies, at all levels.

- Traditionally, changes in one or more of the core competencies can be made through changes in factors among one input group at a time. For instance, the technological competence of an enterprise can be influenced through changes in investments in capital equipment. New raw materials can be introduced through a new technology that improves the overall performance of the product or its manufacturing process. Careful infusion of one or a few individuals—changes in human resources—at selected functions can dramatically change the core competence of an enterprise. All such changes in individual input groups, even though strategically intended to change the core competence, generally result in incremental improvements in outputs. Often such improvements are masked by the noise or variability in the other input categories of the system. On the other hand, a simultaneous change in all four input groupings to achieve a strategic change in core competencies often results in quantum improvements in the output of the system.

- In the System Approach, the macroscopic process measures are truly evidences or means to quantify the core competencies of the enterprise. For instance, measurements of lead-time or on-time delivery may indicate unacceptable performance of individual tasks. Yet, they are not by themselves measures of the performance of the enterprise. In other words, significant changes in lead-time or on-time delivery by itself may not have any impact on increasing shareholder ROI. Conversely, these process measures may indicate the limitations in technology, inadequate global logistics, or poor competency in information automation. Scientists, engineers, and managers all have a responsibility to identify the appropriate internal causal relations, linking the core competencies with the macroscopic process measures.
- The core competencies and the governing internal causal relationships of an enterprise would appear to be unique to that enterprise. Hence, considerable effort is often made to maintain the "secrecy" of the company and its operations. Instead, the core competency of an enterprise and its internal causal relations are indeed the common language that links every individual and every organization within the enterprise. Surprisingly, they are also the

common language that inextricably links the enterprise with the supplier industries as well as the customer industries. Clear and comprehensive understanding of the core competence and the governing internal causal relations leads to extensive and mutual collaboration between these interrelated organizations and industries. Thus, interindustry collaboration and seamless relationships between the supplier industries, the enterprise, and the customer industries is a natural outcome of the System Approach. The redundancy of effort and resources between these interrelated industries can be minimized by active and collaborative learning and by management of the core competencies and the internal causal relations. This concept is illustrated in Figure 4.8.

In this chapter, we have described the enterprise as an input/process/output system. The objective of the System Approach for the management of any enterprise is to maximize the benefit for all stakeholders in the enterprise. These

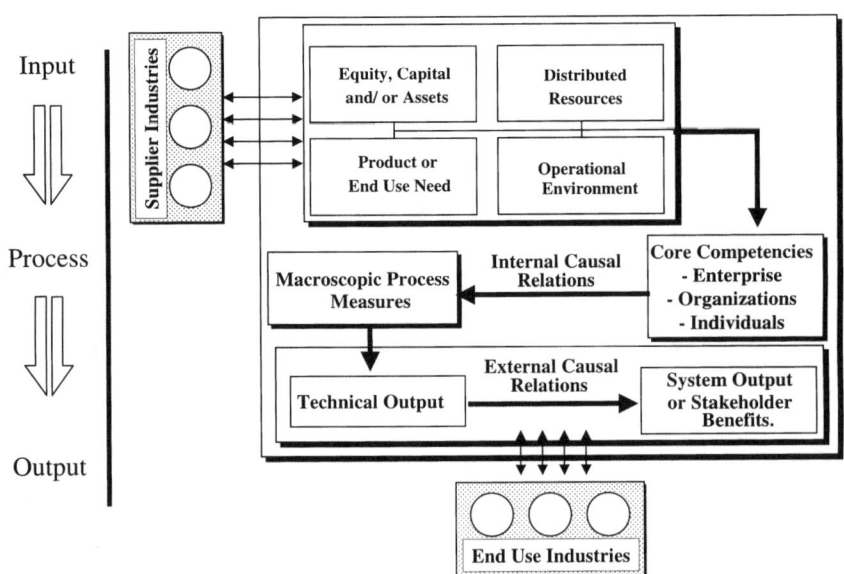

Figure 4.8 • *The System Approach for integration of the enterprise with the supplier and user industries.*

stakeholders are the investors, the employees, supplier industries, end-user industries and the enterprise itself. The benefits to all these stakeholders are defined as the system output. Quantum changes in the system output are necessary for any enterprise that wants to stay competitive in the global economy. Management of any enterprise based on measurements internal to the enterprise (technical outputs) such as sales, profits, market share growth, etc. are indeed very desirable. Nevertheless, such internal measures of the performance of the enterprise alone may no longer be adequate in a global economy.

A traditional view of the enterprise includes hundreds of input parameters and their manipulation, often one or a few at a time. Such manipulation leads only to incremental changes in the output of the system. Frequently, such benefits are masked by the noise or variability in the operation of the system. Fear of "too many changes" permeates the traditional approach to management of the enterprise. As a result, it is recommended that

"managers view each action they take for change as a step on a strategic staircase. Although an organization can seldom attend to more than one campaign for change at a time, it is important to be sure that the next one does not reverse the just completed and dearly won campaign. You must find ways to mount the entire staircase of changes with cumulative effect, rather than simply bumping along the floor. No one solution is the key—the balance required is dynamic and constantly shifting, like riding a bicycle"[13].

In the global economy, the number of input sources and input variables for an enterprise has grown substantially larger than in a traditional economy. Changes in inputs are today being used as individual measures for improving the effectiveness of the individual, organization, or the enterprise. The improvements sought are also focused on limited goals, generally financial and mostly in terms of the parameters internal to the enterprise. Instead, in the System Approach, the changes in the internal causal relations—which are few and well defined—are the common goal of all stakeholders involved in the system. Thus, simultaneous changes in all four input groupings are a logical and coordinated response to the desired changes in the few internal causal relationships.

Management of an enterprise is more than a balancing act. In addition, it is the process of definitive and proactive changes in the internal causal relationships, governed by the few core competencies—technology, information automation, global logistics—and their measurements. These internal causal relations, when they are understood and articulated, become the common language for communication among all stakeholders of the enterprise. Strategic changes in these few internal causal relations lead to changes in the system output. Such strategic changes in internal causal relationships can be affected through simultaneous changes in all four output categories. Such strategic and simultaneous changes in several input factors among all four input categories leads to quantum changes in the system output. Without strategic management of the enterprise as a system, fear of "too many changes" can result, because each change might be viewed as an independent and disconnected action step.

Chapter 5
The System Approach for Industrial Processes

In the previous chapter, we described the enterprise as a system consisting of four input groupings, whose interactions result in few core competencies that can be measured using a number of macroscopic variables. The relationship between the core competencies and their macroscopic measures were described as the "internal causal relations." The enterprise delivers outputs, which can be measured using parameters internal to the enterprise (technical outputs) or as benefits to the stakeholders of the enterprise (system output). The relation between the technical output and the system output is governed by causal relations external to the system, such as the standard of living of the people, national economic policies, etc. Such description of the enterprise as a system lends itself as a powerful means to develop a set of common goals (or common language) for all employees within the enterprise. Such a description of the enterprise also develops a common language that links all stakeholders—the investors, the employees, the end-user industries, the supplier industries, as well as the enterprise itself. In the System Approach, management of the enterprise becomes a matter of modulating the internal causal relations influenced by few core competencies. In the global economy, these core competencies of an enterprise are: technology, information automation, and global logistics. The System Approach also facilitates implementation of the strategy to achieve quantum improvements in the output of the system or benefits for all stakeholders, through simultaneous changes in all four input categories to effect a clear and strategic change in the internal causal relationships.

At first sight, the above description of the enterprise would appear to be of relevance only to corporate managers. On the contrary, the functioning of individual industrial activities can be substantially improved in a manner identical to the approach outlined above for the enterprise as a whole. In the end, every activity in an enterprise becomes the repeated management of the same "system," at a different level, scale, or magnitude. Thus, every employee in the enterprise, from the lowest level to the chief executive, is also involved in the optimization of the same "system."

The above would appear to be a sweeping statement, requiring considerable elaboration. We shall pursue such discussions in the following chapters. In this chapter we will examine the similarities of an enterprise and of the individual industrial activities, each described as an "input/process/output" system. We shall also look at the job or function of each individual as a scaled down version of the enterprise viewed as a system.

For our discussion, let us consider any industrial activity. When reduced to its simplest form, every industrial activity involves the controlled application of energy to convert raw materials into semi-finished goods, components, or finished goods. This conversion or transformation process may occur in one step or in several stages. Every individual step in this transformation process is called a "unit process."[23] (Figure

3.1.a.) An organization consists of many such unit processes, carried out in desired combinations (series, parallel, or any combination) as illustrated in Figure 3.1.b. The unit processes do not function by themselves. They require activities or functions, which transfer input resources into the process. They also require management of information pertaining to the process and the transfer events. This description of the process along with the transfer events and the information management was described earlier (Figure 2.4). The purpose served by the "unit process" may vary depending on the focus or primary thrust of the organizational entity employing the unit process. Thus, an enterprise consists of many organizations, each with its own set of unit processes (Figure 3.1.c). It is likely that many of the organizations within an enterprise would have several of the unit processes repeated or duplicated. Ultimately, the technologies governing the various unit processes become the core technology, one of the core competencies of the enterprise. Similarly, the information (collection, dissemination, and manipulation) and logistics or transfer events linking various unit processes become the other two core competencies of the enterprise. In the global economy, the activities pertaining to information can be automated in a manner not conceived of in the past. We call this "information automation." Similarly, the transfer events (logistics) of the past were limited to local events. Today, thanks to "global logistics," transfer events of every kind can be linked to resources anywhere in the world on both the input as well as the output side of the unit process. This orderly assemblage of unit processes, individuals, and their organization, is collectively represented as the enterprise.

The preponderance of a few unit processes repeated many times through several organizations within an enterprise is worth some clarification. Consider, for example, "grinding" as a unit industrial process. In its simplest description, "grinding" is a surface generation process using abrasives as cutting edges. This unit process is employed by a variety of industries to generate a range of desired surfaces on a wide range of components and on a wide range of work materials. Yet, the basic unit process is the generation of surfaces through the application of energy delivered to the surface generation process through the engineered composite—the abrasive product—with its abrasive cutting edges. This unit process may be employed in the research department (for evaluation of new process configurations), in the design and process development functions (to specify desired surface features and how to achieve them), or in a diversity of configurations on the manufacturing floor. Nonetheless, the chosen unit process at its most elementary level can be repeatedly observed within an organization (research, manufacturing, etc.) and in an assemblage of organizations (called the enterprise). Ultimately, stripped of these internal boundaries, the enterprise is a collection of unit processes governed by the core technology and the processing of information (information automation) and the transfer of resources (logistics) into and out of the unit processes. Stripped of its internal organizational boundaries, the enterprise is an assemblage of unit processes to deploy the core competencies to transform the inputs into value/benefits for the stakeholders of the enterprise.

Now, let's return to the detailed understanding of any unit process. Too frequently, the process is treated as a "black box." Sometimes this "black box" approach is replaced by an attempt to measure the "process." Then correlations are sought between these measured parameters. The process is managed to retain the parameters between set limits. This methodology is frequently referred to as "Statistical Process Control." As discussed in an earlier chapter, statistical process control (SPC) is an excellent tool for maintaining a process within set limits. It is capable of delivering continuous improvements, as long as the "process" remains stable and not vulnerable to frequent requirements for change. In the global economy, quantum improvements are constantly required along with a need for flexibility, agility, and responsiveness to change. This requirement appears to be in conflict with SPC, as it is generally practiced.

No industrial process can be successful if it is not maintained and managed within controlled limits. Hence, it is not intended or implied to lessen the value or impact of statistical process control. But, too frequently, SPC has become an exit vehicle for both engineers and managers to skip the comprehensive understanding of the scientific fundamentals or core technology behind the unit processes. Without such focus on core technology, statistical experiments and control procedures set in motion a series of irreversible steps or tasks that collectively become both indispensable and expensive over a period of time. An organization burdened with these limitations is easily displaced by a competitive response, often based on changes in the core technology or a better adaptation of the same core technology, with quantum changes in the process outputs. However, the statistical process control methods are indispensable to retain the process within consistent limits or set points, until a set point or quantum change in the core technology is identified.

Every unit process consists of a large number of input factors as well as output factors. A typical example of these input and output factors for any industrial unit process is shown in Figure 5.1. These inputs can be divided into four distinct categories.

Machine tool or platform. It is the platform, or equipment, that enables the occurrence of the unit process. This input category is associated with capital or the investment of large sums of money. Such inputs to the process are often discrete in nature. The machine tool by itself does not accomplish the unit process. Instead, the unit process is made possible through tools, instruments, or accessories, which work in conjunction with the machine tool.

Processing tools. The process is accomplished on the machine tool platform with the aid of tools, jigs and fixtures, work holders, etc. They work in conjunction with the machine tool. We shall call them processing tools or "distributed resources." Frequently they are referred to as tooling, consumables, commodities, etc. These processing tools also include "tooling" or

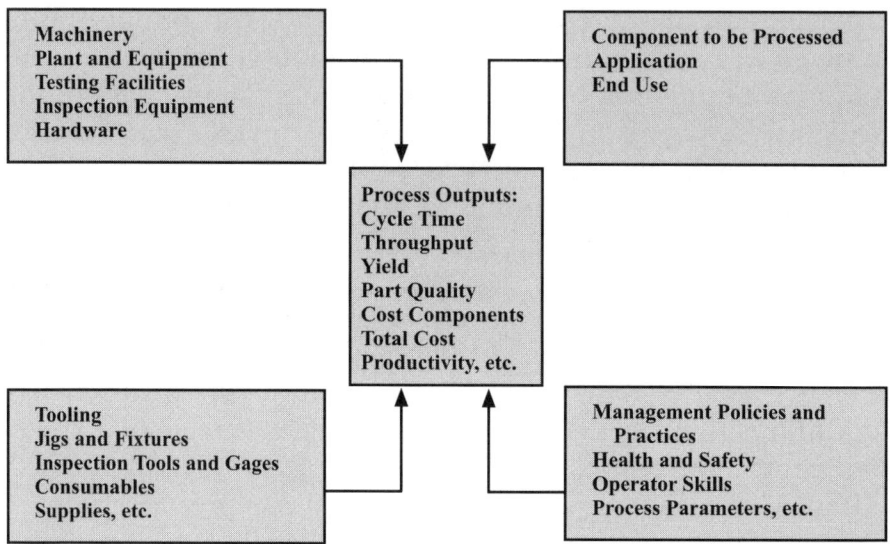

Figure 5.1 • Typical input/output factors for any industrial/manufacturing process.[1]

[1]The above are selected examples and not all inclusive.

"consumables" used to transfer the inputs into the "process." They also include tooling or consumables used to transfer and/or verify the outputs of the unit process. Typically, for every machine tool engaged in a unit process, there are tens to hundreds of distributed resources used in that process!

Workpiece or application. The unit process is carried out on the workpiece or application. This is often the only input category that the end-user of the unit process is actively familiar with.

Operational factors. The above three input groupings are brought together under certain process parameters or operational factors. These are variables set or changed at the operating level or on the shop floor, where the unit process is practiced. Invariably, the operational factors affect or influence all the other input factors simultaneously. Thus, all three of the above input categories bring with them an ability to influence the choice of the operational factors. This interconnection between the four input categories becomes evident only when the unit process is viewed as a whole or as a system.

Thus, all inputs to any unit process can be classified under these four input groupings: Machine tool, processing tools/distributed resources, work material, and operational factors. A typical example of these four input groupings for several manufacturing unit processes is shown in Table 5.1.

The detail with which an input category is considered largely depends on our purpose relative to the unit process. As an example, the typical input parameters for "grinding" as a manufacturing unit process are shown in Figure 5.2. A carefully detailed analysis can identify several hundred input parameters for each industrial unit process. In the task-oriented approach, individuals are assigned responsibility for one or perhaps a few of these parameters. Indeed, it will not come as

Table 5.1
Typical input parameters for various unit processes.[1]

Unit Process	Machine Tool	Processing Tool	Work Material/ Application	Operational Factors
Machining	Lathe	Cutting Tools	Component	Speed, Feed, D.O.C., etc.
Grinding	Grinding M/C	Abrasive Tools	Component	Wheel Speed, Work Speed, Stock Removed, etc.
Forming	Forming Machine	Forming Die	Component	Speed, Reduction Ratio, etc.
Pressing	Pressing Machine	Pressing Tools	Powder Mix	Pressure, Area, Volume, etc.
Sintering	Sintering Furnace	Sintering Tools	Component	Temperature, Pressure, Sintering Atmosphere, etc.
Forging	Forging Press	Forging Tools	Component	Temperature, Pressure, etc.
Casting	Foundry	Casting Tools	Casting	Temperature, Cooling, etc.
EDM	Elec. Discharge Machine	Electrode	Component	Voltage, Current, etc.
ECM	Elec. Chemical Machining Tool	Electrolyte	Component	Current, Current Density, P_n, etc.
Vacuum Deposition Processes	Vacuum Furnace	Electrodes, Gages, etc.	Component	Voltage, Temperature, Pressure, Target Distance, etc.

(1) The above are extremely few variables selected for examples only and are not all-inclusive.

102 • The System Approach

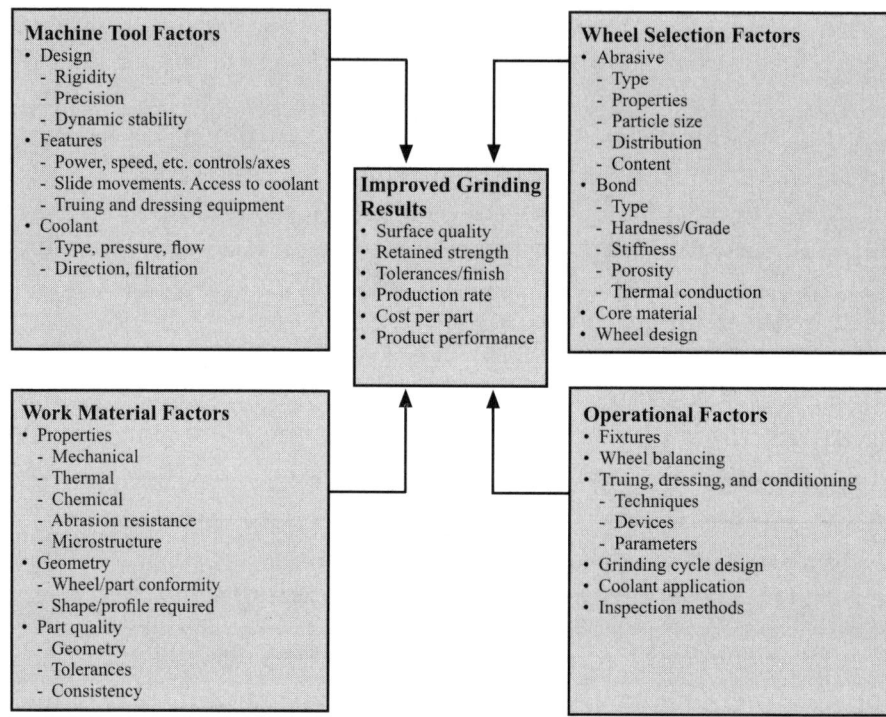

[1] The above are selected examples of parameters influencing the grinding processes; not all inclusive.

Figure 5.2 • *Selected engineering parameters[1] or variables influencing a specific industrial/manufacturing process. (e.g., grinding process).*

a surprise to find individuals in the research community who specialize in one or a few of these parameters as part of their life-long study.

In earlier chapters we noted that addressing specific or individual components of a problem, described as a task, is no longer sufficient to be competitive in the global marketplace. This is indeed true for individuals (as employees) as much as it is true for enterprises (as employers). The system description of the unit process helps to define the problem as a whole. In this approach, the unit process is identified through the governing "microscopic process interactions." These are the physical phenomena brought into action by the collection of several inputs classified under four input groupings: machine tool, processing tools, work material, or application and operational factors (Figure 5.3). The measurement of the microscopic interactions occurs through a set of variable parameters called macroscopic variables. The physical phenomena (microscopic interactions) when influenced by the inputs, result in outputs in terms that are relevant to the organization employing the unit process (called technical output). When described as a whole, the unit process becomes an input/process/output system governed by a few internal causal relationships. These internal causal relationships define the science of the process (called "scientific principles"). The output expectations—the system output—become apparent when the system is viewed with a perspective far removed from its day-to-day operations. Value/benefit relationships, or causal relations extrinsic to the "process," determine the relationships between the technical and the system outputs.

The System Approach helps to define the problem precisely, in a common language, so that it becomes of immediate interest to everyone participating in the unit process. The physical

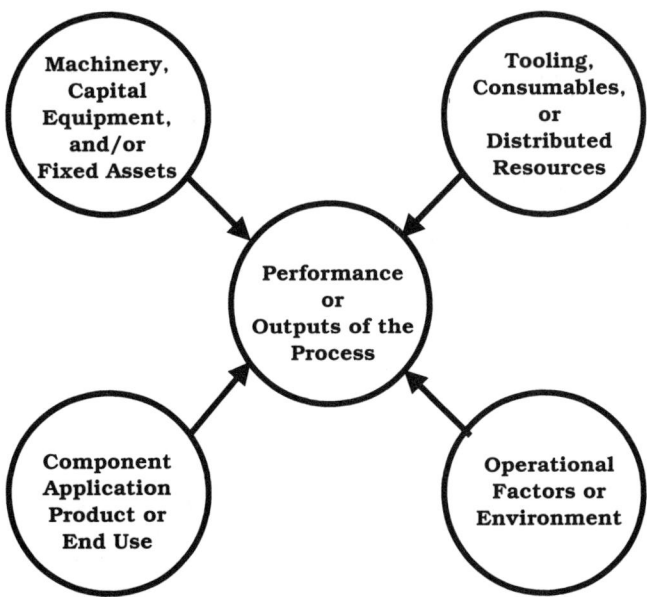

Figure 5.3 • *Industrial unit processes viewed as an input/ouput system.*

phenomena defining the unit process provide the common language. (Figure 5.4.) It (or they) knows no organizational boundaries or geographic barriers. For instance, a certain combination of input variables will result in the same engineering result (technical output) irrespective of the location where the process is carried out (in any organization within an enterprise, or any geography in the world!). The interpretation of the engineering results (technical output) in terms of its value to the enterprise (system output) will, of course, vary based on economic considerations pertinent to the enterprise, industry, its geography, etc. As an example, the "cycle time" in the manufacture of a component is a technical output. The cycle time in parts per hour has the same meaning independent of the location where the unit process is carried out. Yet, the value/benefit of the "cycle time" will vary depending on the economic factors. The monetary cost (value) of the "cycle time" is far lower in developing countries compared to developed countries due to the local economic factors such as labor cost, capital cost, etc. Even within a country, the "cycle time" may

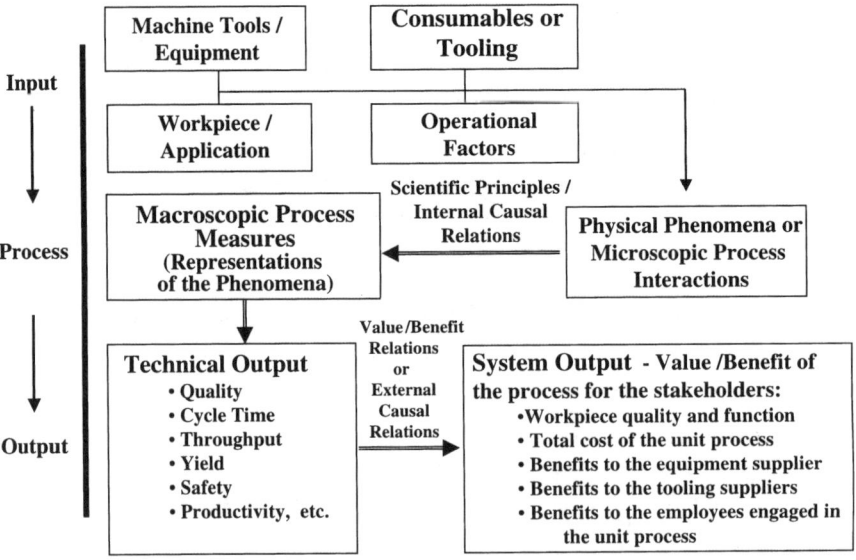

Figure 5.4 • *The system approach for industrial processes.*

have different costs, depending on how critically the process is needed. The value of the "cycle time" will also vary within a plant, depending on available capacity, rate limiting process steps, etc. Thus the "system output" can be distinguished from the "technical output" of the system through causal relationships or influences external to the unit process.

Every unit industrial process can be defined as an exploitation of certain physical phenomena amenable to specific scientific principles or causal relations. This is one of the core competencies we deploy whenever the unit process is used, which we shall call the "science" of the unit process.

No industrial activity is commercially relevant unless the inputs are brought to bear in an organized manner and the performance of the process is "measured" and "monitored," leading to the desired outputs of the process. This deployment of resources in all four input categories, dedicated to exploiting the physical phenomena in order to achieve the desired commercially viable output, is called "engineering."

Both the physical phenomena (science) and its deployment (engineering) are of no significance unless they are rendered in a manner that provides value to the enterprise. This process of determining the "relative worth" of a unit process and realizing such value (often in terms of time and money) is called "management." The process of planning, organization, and coordination of the resources and the verification of the output against set goals (control) is also frequently referred to as "management."

The successful deployment of the System Approach for unit industrial processes requires the simultaneous consideration of these three core competencies: "science," "engineering," and "management." (Figure 5.5.) The term "simultaneous consideration" is very critical here. Driven by globalization, the need for simultaneity between engineering and management is now widely recognized. Concurrent engineering is often thought of as a tool to create this simultaneous consideration. However, concurrent engineering by itself will be insufficient, unless the third core competence, "science," is also brought into simul-

106 • The System Approach

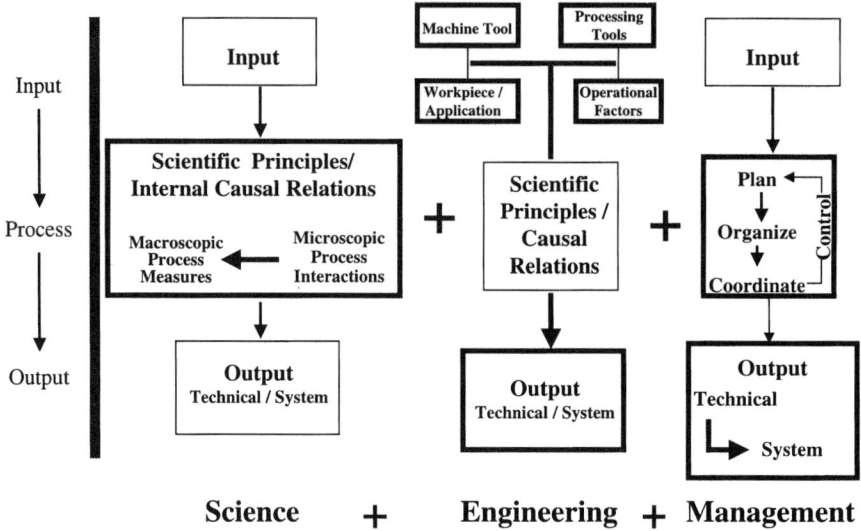

Figure 5.5 • *The system approach for industrial processes requires the simultaneous deployment of three core competencies: science, engineering and management.*

taneous consideration in the deployment of unit processes in industrial activities.

At the outset, this will appear to be a formidable task. In current (traditional) industrial organizations, everyone is a task-oriented individual facilitating certain aspects of "science," "engineering," or "management." As individuals gain responsibility for a group or collection of tasks, they become classified as scientists, engineers, and/or managers. Untold difficulties are being experienced in the current efforts for concurrent engineering where engineers from different departments are required to think and function on behalf of each other. Processes and tools of information automation are bringing the concurrency between departments together. In all of this, "management" is finding that its role is to facilitate such concurrent activities between departments (aided by information automation and utilizing resources from worldwide sources—global logistics). Recent gains in the U.S. industry—reflected as productivity enhancement—have been achieved largely through such simultaneous consideration of engineering and management activities, aided by information automation and global logistics. The integration of "science" as a concurrent part of the industrial process is still a long way off. It is very much limited to research laboratories and academic studies at this time.

As described earlier (and depicted in Figure 3.1.b), any organization can be defined as an entity that deploys a selected number of unit processes. Hence, any organization is a collective representation of the "input/process/output" systems representing the individual unit processes deployed by the organization. This systems description of an organization, governed by its core competencies of science, engineering, and management deployed through the unit processes, is shown in Figure 5.6. Information automation and global logistics, which are the core competencies of the enterprise, are also the underlying core competencies of the organization (as a subset of the enterprise). In addition, these two core competencies also play a role in the interconnection between the unit processes deployed by the organization.

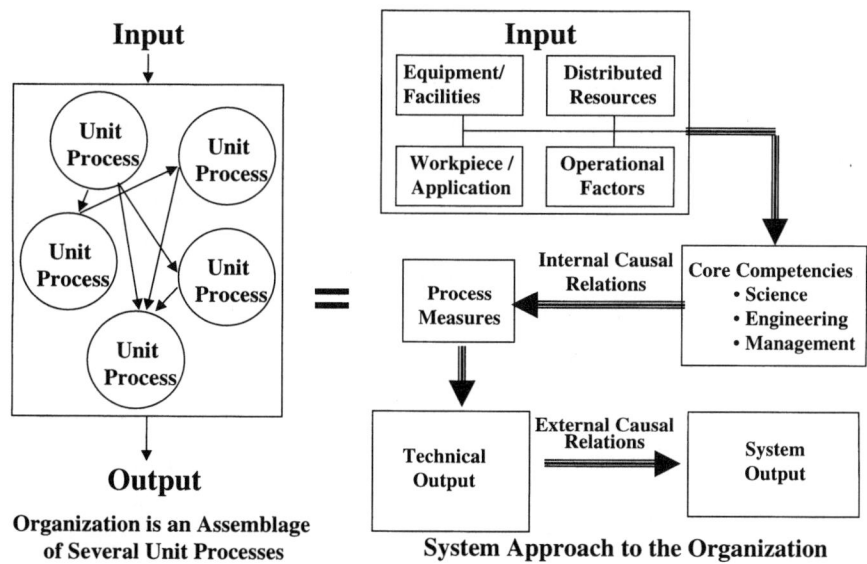

Figure 5.6 • Industrial organization and the System Approach.

Having defined the "unit process" as an input/process/output system, let us now focus our attention on the benefits of such a "System Approach."

- The system description of the unit process facilitates identification of all input variables under four broad groups, (i.e.) platform/machine tool, processing tools/distributed resources, workpiece/application and operational factors. This classification of inputs to the unit process is essential, and all inputs must be adequately considered. Each of the input groups also represents organizations, enterprises, or supplier industries that are outside of the unit process, but have a key influence on the successful accomplishment of the unit process. Without such classification of the input factors, any attempt to improve or influence the unit process is often mired with redundant discussions and considerations, which can at best be described as "opinions" and "judgments."
- Besides facilitating a thorough consideration of all the input factors, the System Approach is also beneficial to achieving quantum improvements in the system output. Changes in all four input categories, which strategically influence the scientific principles or causal relation, always have a large scale or quantum impact on the output of the system. Therefore, changes in many of the input factors can be simultaneously implemented based on a single (or a few) scientific/causal relation. This minimizes the need for repeated trial and error in the improvement of the unit process.
- Changes in one (or a few) input parameter, even though implemented based on strategic consideration of scientific principles/causal relations, often results in incremental improvements in the output of the system. But, frequently, even such incremental improvements may be lost due to the influence of variations in the other input factors. In a global competitive environment, such incremental improvements and their associated uncertainties are not sufficient or acceptable.

As an example, consider the development of a new machine tool that can influence a specific causal relation (based on scientific principles) pertinent to a unit process. Introduction of such a new machine tool to the marketplace is difficult at best, as the benefits to be accomplished are incremental in nature. However, if the intended change in the causal relation can be brought about by simultaneous and appropriate changes in the processing tools, workpiece properties and operational factors, the changes in output are large scale or quantum in nature. Such large-scale improvements are also very much in need in the global competitive environment.

Simultaneous change in more than one input group would appear to be counter to common practices. In the era of task-oriented management of activities, we are frequently reminded "not to change more than one thing at a time." In the absence of an understanding of the scientific principles/causal relations, each change in input factor is perceived as a change to the unit process. However, a comprehensive understanding of the scientific principles/causal relations governing the unit process permits one to view many changes in each of the four input groupings as leading to a single strategic change in the pertinent scientific/causal relation governing the process. The cumulative and synergistic effect of all these changes in all four input groupings is also very much needed, as it leads to quantum improvements in the process output. The internal causal relations governing the unit process permits one to view many changes in each of the four input groupings as leading to a single strategic change in the pertinent scientific/causal relation governing the process.

- By defining the unit process as a "system," the pertinent physical phenomena or the key microscopic process interactions are clearly identified and put to use by all involved.
- The measurements of the process (macroscopic variables), and their linkage to the microscopic process interactions, becomes the next critical step in the description of the unit process as a "system." Any measurement of the process should be to help elucidate the microscopic

interactions. Such clear causal connection between the process interaction (the phenomena) and its measurement defines the extent of our understanding of the process (in terms of the scientific principles/causal relations). It is worth quoting a popular adage, "hundreds of data points do not equal a single conclusion." Indeed, such clear causal relations between observations (macroscopic process variables) and their relation to the physical phenomena (microscopic process interaction) creates the concurrency in thought process between the "science" and "engineering" aspects pertinent to the process. Clear and comprehensive understanding of the scientific principles/causal relations permits the identification of a few critical necessary process measurements. The engineering understanding of such causal relations creates the means for their adequate measurements. Such causal relations, when they are identified on a manufacturing shop floor, are called "solutions to production problems." If they are present in a laboratory environment, we call them "process simulation." An engineer with comprehensive understanding of the scientific principles identifies the few critical process interactions and the parameters to be measured on the shop floor and is also able to reproduce the same physical phenomena in terms of process interactions in a controlled environment—the laboratory—to better understand the process or evaluate the means to achieve desired changes in the process. Such a professional involved with a unit process can easily migrate between research, process development, manufacturing engineering, and shop floor operations. Such migration between the various organizations of the enterprise is made possible through the commonality of the scientific principles, their measurements, and replication of the process interactions or causal relationships.

- The scientific principles/internal causal relations of the unit process provide the common language that pertains to everyone involved in the process. Supplier industries have to conform to these scientific principles. The user industries have to rely on the same scientific principles in their use of the "unit process" to achieve their desired benefits. This connectivity between the supplier industries and the end-user industries through the "unit process" viewed as a system is shown in Figure 5.7. Such an interrelated view of the unit process leads to natural and mutual collaboration between related industries and the enterprise employing the unit process. Similarly, related organizations (such as research, engineering, process development, manufacturing, etc.) come together through the common language of scientific principles/ internal causal relations pertinent to the unit process. Such a System Approach facilitates concurrent engineering based on scientific principles or cause and effect reasoning. Such concurrency in the functioning of related industries and/or related functions inside an enterprise is very much the need for success in the global economy.

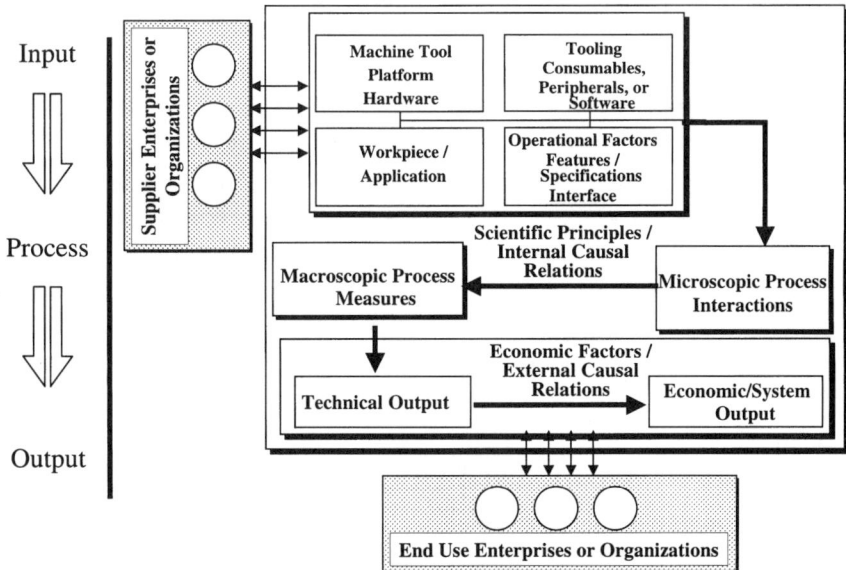

Figure 5.7 • *System Approach for integration of the unit process or the organization using it, with the supplier and user enterprises and/or organizations.*

- The System Approach to unit processes is not a mere exercise in organizing pertinent input factors and the governing scientific/causal relations. Instead, such logical connection between the input factors and the principles governing their interactions leads to a comprehensive understanding of the consequences of the process or the output of the system. Such consequences are further divided between the engineering or technical outputs and their value/benefit or economic consequence, described as the system output.

The objective of the System Approach is to achieve quantum improvements in the output of the system or its economic benefits. Such quantum improvements are brought about by simultaneous changes in all four input groups, based on strategic changes in single or a few scientific principles.

In addition to the overarching objective of large scale or quantum improvements in the output, the System Approach provides a number of other practical benefits. Description of the unit process as a "system" by itself helps to define the "problem" in a comprehensive manner. Otherwise, the industrial environment is generally complicated with descriptions of the "process" from a number of different perspectives. The researcher or scientist describes the process in terms of "scientific descriptions." The engineer describes the "process" in terms of the parameter he/she is familiar with. There is a description of the problem from a sales engineering perspective, which is different from the machine tool procurement perspective. There are even differences in the description of the process by the tooling engineer, the materials engineer, and so forth. Yet, the unit process is the same. In the global economy, a single engineer is often required to handle all facets of the "unit process" as well as its economic justification! In such a scenario of diminishing resources, the expectation to achieve greater overall benefits is also increasing. It is this squeeze between the need for greater output with diminishing resources to achieve the same results that has been named "productivity enhancement." The System Approach provides a logical means to handle this growing expectation by facilitating a thought process that is simultaneously scientific, engineering oriented, cost effective, and management oriented.

At the most elementary level, the System Approach permits the true assessment of our understanding of the problem. For example, all discussions about a "unit process" can be captured as factors or information pertaining to one or the other box shown in Figure 5.4. When used as a working tool, it will not be surprising to find out that, after hours of discussion, only one or a few boxes of the input/process/output system will have been addressed. On many occasions, the empty boxes will indicate inputs needed from sources that are part of the system, but are not part presently of the discussion. The description of the "process," when complete, will often be the same, at the lowest level in the organization to the highest level. The differences will merely be the scale or magnitude of the input factors considered, as well as the scale or magnitude of the output. But the microscopic interactions and their representation or manifestation through the macroscopic variables will remain the same at all levels of consideration of the unit process. Thus, the System Approach reduces the industrial problem from hundreds of opinions and judgments to one of a few basic principles verifiable through a limited number of measurements or data sets.

Thus far, we have described how an organization is composed of several unit processes deployed in any unique combination pertinent to the organization. The enterprise itself is a collection of organizations. We have also described the unit process as a "system." In the case of unit processes (and hence the organization employing them), the core competencies governing the system are science, engineering, and management. In the case of enterprise, the same core competencies present themselves as technology, information automation, and global logistics. This transition between core competencies of a unit process and that of an enterprise is recognized when we look at the meaning of the words such as technology, logistics, and automation. Each of these terms represents some combination of science, engineering, and management.

The term "management" itself is worth some discussion in the context of the System Approach. Due to a systematic development of specialized skills, the term "management" has come to be viewed as distinct and separate from engineering. Too frequently, engineers view their jobs as involving individual tasks to be accomplished alone or with a team of specialists. At the end of the day, "management" is nothing more than a process to "plan," "organize," "coordinate," and "control" any activity to achieve the desired end result. This process is often called "operations management." Frequently, time and cost are associated with the expected end-result. The verification process and feedback to achieve the end-results are generally called "controls." But there could be no activity without the involvement of a "management" component. Management as a core competence is inherent with the desire for "problem-solving." Management is the methodical problem solving process, with an eye on the end-result. Thus, the management function is not the responsibility of the "managers" alone. It is indeed the job of everyone. The core competencies of management, their meaning, and the common tools used to measure them, are described in Table 5.2.

Management is also the aspect of the problem solving process that addresses questions such as: "Why we are interested in the process?" Or, "What can we get out of the technical aspects of the process?" The search for "Why?" is frequently termed as "strategic thinking" or "strategic management." Such considerations of management as a core competence are also highlighted in Figure 5.5.

Thus far, we have described industrial processes purely in terms of activities and their representation as a system. But industrial activities are intimately linked to individuals at every level of the enterprise. Industrial activities do not come about on their own. They are conceived, implemented, deployed, and exploited by individuals (employees) to serve the needs of the stakeholders of the enterprise. Here we do not refer to employees only as blue-collar workers, employed for

TABLE 5.2.
Core competencies of management.

Management Activity	What Does it Mean?	Macroscopic Process Measures (or) Common Tools
• Plan	A scheme, method, or design to achieve the end result.	Vision Strategy Goals Objectives
• Organize	To bring together (arrange systematically) the resources required to execute the plan.	Programs Projects Budgets Assignments
• Coordinate	To bring into harmonious relation or action, integrated action or interactions. Not subordination.	Schedules Meetings Discussions Reports
• Control	To check or verify against the plan. Restrain or regulate. Conformance of objectives. Not mere exercise of authority.	Measurements Reviews Rewards Recognition

their physical effort or skills. Nor do we refer to employees as white-collar workers, employed for processing of information or facilitating the logistics. As we have discussed in earlier chapters, both types of traditional employments are gradually diminishing in the global economy. Yet enterprises, their organization, and the unit processes, are comprised of people who manage the science and engineering aspects of the unit processes. These are the "knowledge workers." But knowledge by itself is not adequate, if it is not deployed to achieve useful end result. The outcome of such deployment of knowledge is called "experience." Just as the unit processes are combined to produce an organization, individuals and their interaction lead to an industrial organization. Thus, individual workers who possess knowledge and experience are also required to possess skills that will allow them to effectively interact with each other. These are commonly known as "people skills." These core competencies are measured in a number of ways depending on the industrial activity engaged in by the individual. (Table 5.3.) Thus, a systems description of the individual's contribution to any industrial activity, organization, or enterprise may be described as shown in Figure 5.8. This figure also shows the enterprise, organization, and the individuals, each comprised of a "system" with well-defined core competencies, found in any industrial activity. Thus, individuals in any industrial activity in the global economy may also be perceived of as input/process/output transformers, with input constraints and output requirements. This input/process/output expectation for any individual in a globalized economy is shown in Figure 5.9.

Industrial activity as a problem solving process has thus far been described at three distinct levels: the enterprise, the organization, and the individual. Core competencies for each of these organizational subsets have been described. (Figure 5.8.) It should be made clear that what we have described here as core competencies is nothing new. Until now such core competencies at every level could be deployed individually or in some arbitrary combination. This is the case in many situations. But, thanks to globalization, such arbitrary choices or strengths in core competencies are no longer adequate. Indeed, what is required is a synergistic deployment of all three-core competencies at every level. This transformation process from a traditional enterprise to a globalized enterprise is shown in Figure 5.10.

In the System Approach, the organization is a microcosm of the enterprise and the individual is a microcosm on the organization. The distinctions are primarily in the assemblage of core competencies. Each level is an assemblage of core competencies from the level below it. In the traditional or task-oriented enterprise, any arbitrary combination of core competence at any of the three levels—individual, organization, and the enterprise—was adequate. However, in a global economy there is a need for synergistic and simultaneous deployment of all three core competencies at every one of the three levels. Viewed from the human resource perspective, these three levels are: individuals, organization, and enterprise. Viewed from the point of industrial activities, the three levels are: unit process, organization, and enterprise. The core competencies

The System Approach for Industrial Processes • 117

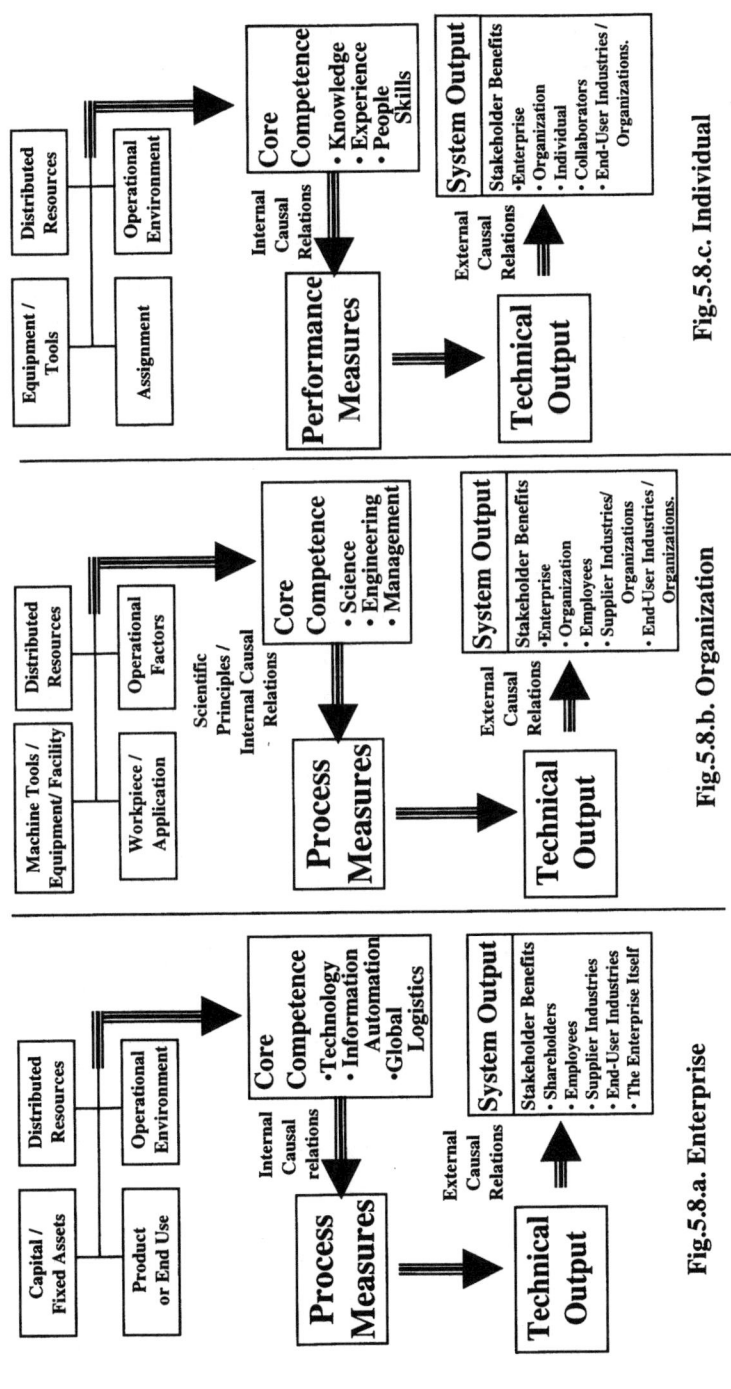

Figure 5.8 • The System Approach for performance of the enterprise, organization or individuals in the global economy.

are required to be deployed, at each level, synergistically and in appropriate balance, with the level above, depending on the nature of the rapidly changing marketplace. This gradual

TABLE 5.3.
Core Competencies of Individuals.

Core Competencies and Motives of Individuals	What Does it Mean?	Macroscopic Process Measures (or) Common Tools
• Knowledge	Deep and extensive learning; well informed. Comprehension of various aspects of the subject.	Education Reading Learning from Peers Observations
• Experience	Skill derived from actual participation or direct training. Accumulated opinions and judgments.	Hands-on Activity Involvement Experiments Risk Taking
• People Skills	Ability to seek out others and receive their support. Help and cooperation. Willingness to reciprocate; to achieve mutual benefits.	Honesty Integrity Communication Team Spirit

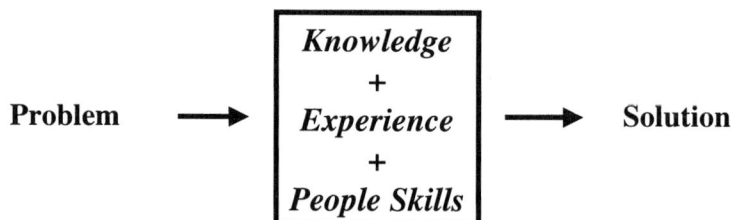

Problem → *Knowledge + Experience + People Skills* → **Solution**

- Fewer Jobs
- Multiple Tasks Per Person
- Global Competition for Currently Available Jobs
- Advances in Information Technology have Eliminated Large Numbers of White-Collar Jobs

- Awareness of the Industrial Activity as Input/Process/Output System
- Orientation for Problem Resolution vs. Task-Orientation
- Quantum Improvements in Output per Employee
- Interdisciplinary Thought Process

Figure 5.9 • Individual employee as a "problem solver" in the context of global economy.

transition from the traditional or task-orientation to the integrated, entrepreneurial, or system-orientation, is shown in Figure 5.10.

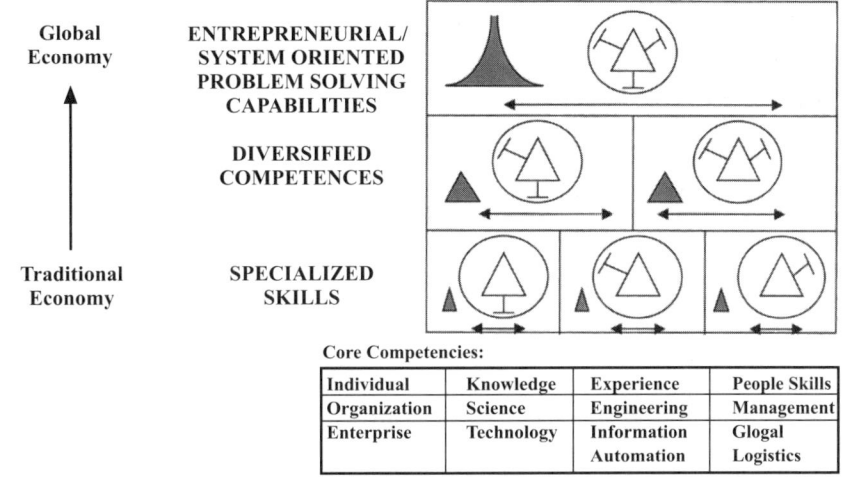

Figure 5.10 • *Synergistic development of core competencies of individuals, organization and the enterprise using the System Approach.*

Chapter 6
The System Approach as a Strategic Tool in the Global Economy

Whether we take a "top down" approach from the enterprise to individual workers, or a "bottom up" approach from unit processes and their progressive assemblage into organization and ultimately the enterprise as a whole, the resulting activity at every level becomes representative of the input/process/output system. As we outlined in Chapter 4, all industrial activities performed by individuals, organizations, or enterprises can be represented as an input/process/output system. In Chapter 5, we saw that all industrial activities, composed of unit processes and their assemblage, leading to organization and the enterprise as a whole, are also amenable to treatment as input/process/output systems. The System Approach merely recognizes the input/process/output system as the basic description of all our industrial activities. In this chapter, we shall illustrate several additional practical implications and uses or benefits of the System Approach.

122 • The System Approach

All individuals in the industrial society are trained to work and function systematically, following set rules and guidelines to execute clearly laid-out tasks. The need for a systematic approach has always been there and necessary. The System Approach should be distinguished clearly from the systematic pursuit of activities. The System Approach calls for the understanding that all industrial activities are representations of input/process/output systems. Strategic use of such systems is achieved by effective deployment of core competencies, the objective being quantum changes in the system output (or benefits to all stakeholders in the process).

Consider the observations of the chief of an enterprise, evaluating the enterprise in the context of globalization.

1. The assessment of the enterprise starts with the description of the enterprise as a system. (Figure 4.4.)
2. The input factors to the enterprise are classified as capital/fixed assets, distributed or variable resources, products or end use served by the enterprise, and the operational environment. The degree of clarity and ease with which the input factors can be sorted among these four input groups reflects the comprehension of the enterprise and its functions. Such classification also helps to identify related industries, both suppliers as well as end-users contributing to the input categories with which the enterprise is integrally linked. The collective success of these groups of enterprises is integrally linked to the success of the individual enterprises.
3. The process measures are studied carefully. They are evaluated to establish how well they measure or represent the core competencies of the enterprise—technology, information automation, and global logistics. The effective use of process measures and their relationship to the core competencies reflects the ability and understanding of the enterprise in terms of its internal causal relations. These internal causal relations also provide the basis for developing seamless relationships with the supplier industries as well as the customer or end-user

industries. (Figure 4.8.)
4. The output measures are studied and assessed as to how well they reflect measures of interest to those close to the daily activities of the enterprise (technical output) versus measures of interest to all stakeholders of the enterprise (system output). The relationships between the technical outputs and the system outputs are determined by the external causal relationships. These external relationships establish the connection between the outputs of the enterprise and their value/benefit, as viewed by the stakeholders of the enterprise.
5. Thus, the enterprise is assessed as a system with a comprehensive view of the inputs, internal causal relations, and external causal relations.

    Then, the chief of the enterprise can proceed to establish the goals for quantum changes in the output of the enterprise necessary to survive and succeed in the global competitive environment.
6. To the extent that these goals are linked to the system output and not restricted to the technical output, the more likely will be the long-term success of the enterprise and all its stakeholders.
7. If changes are sought in all four input groupings, with a strategic intent to change the core competencies (and verified through clearly defined macroscopic process measures), then quantum change in system output is the most likely outcome. If changes are sought in one of the four input groupings at a time, the output will always be incremental and often insufficient to meet the global competitive challenges.
8. To the extent such a system description of the enterprise is understood by each and every employee of the enterprise, the more coherent and competitive will be the enterprise as a whole in the era of globalization. This viewpoint is schematically illustrated in Figure 6.1.

    The core competencies of individuals, organizations, and the enterprise have existed all along and will con-

124 • The System Approach

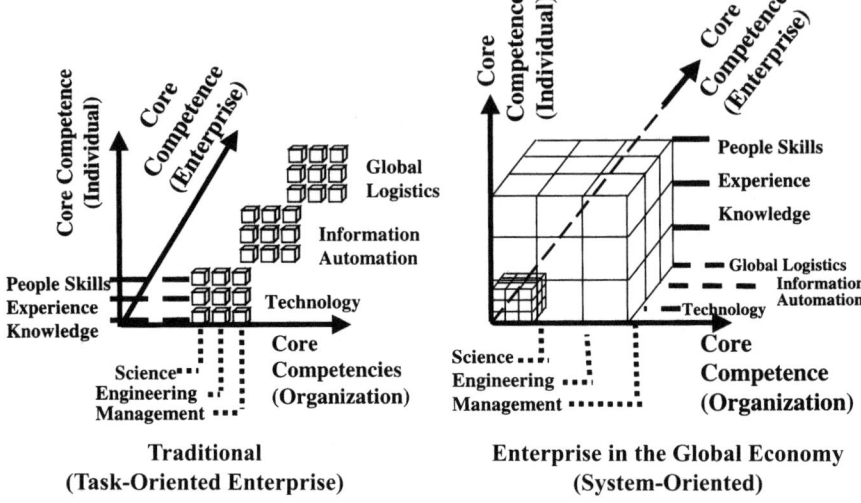

Figure 6.1 • *System Approach—An integration of core competencies of individuals, organizations, and the enterprise.*

tinue to exist. The traditional enterprise with a task-orientation deploys these core competencies as individual or isolated competencies. The individual, organization, or enterprise that creates the most desirable combination at a given moment, is considered successful. Frequently, these combinations of core competencies in the traditional enterprise are at best two-dimensional in nature. In the system-oriented global enterprise, the core competencies of individuals, organizations, and the enterprise are identical and always three-dimensional in nature. Thus, the individual, organization and enterprise are always a progression of the same three-dimensional module of core competencies. However, the evidences of the impact of these core competencies are observed and measured through knowledge, experience, and people skills at the individual level, through science, engineering, and management at the organizational level, and through technology, information automation, and global logistics at the enterprise level. This progression of synergistic growth in core competencies from the individual to the enterprise is shown in Figure 6.2. The impact of such progression in terms of the twin requirements in the global economy—agility and effectiveness—is also shown in this figure.

9. Finally, every reproduction of this system is a growth opportunity for the individuals, organization, and/or the enterprise. If the scale of the system is small and number the of replications is large, the enterprise gives the impression of being agile, flexible, and entrepreneurial, which are qualities very much needed for survival and success in the global marketplace. The advances in information automation and global logistics permit such replications of the enterprise systems to be easier than ever before. We shall further discuss this aspect later in this chapter.

Now, let's reverse the situation and look at the enterprise from the view of the individual employee in the enterprise.

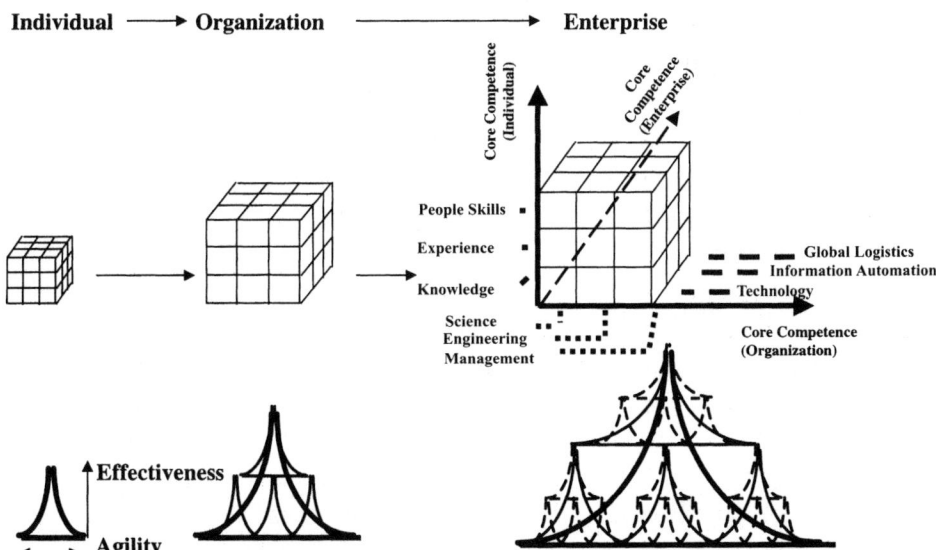

Figure 6.2 • System Approach—synergistic evolution of competencies of individuals, organizations, and the enterprise necessary for success in the global economy.

126 • The System Approach

The process of assessment would be the same in the System Approach.
1. There should be a comprehensive description of the enterprise as a system by the employee in order to permit a clear view of the core competencies of the enterprise and of the organization. This, in turn, leads to a logical connection with the individual's core competencies in terms of knowledge, experience, and people skills. The alignment of these individual core competencies with those of the organization (science, engineering, and management) and, finally, the core competencies of the enterprise that the individual is a part of (technology, information automation, and global logistics) is the challenge posed for every individual to survive and succeed in the era of globalization.
2. To the extent that there is congruence between the view of the enterprise as a system as perceived by the employer versus the system view of the enterprise, as perceived by the employee, there will be synergy and effectiveness between the employee and the employer. (Figure 6.2.)
3. It is clear that the enterprise may be viewed as a system, from top down or from the bottom up. Developing consistency between these two views of the enterprise as a system is the key to each individual's career development in the era of global economy. It is also key for the employers in their effective development of all components of the enterprise, organizations, and individuals. Such synergistic development in both directions is a key requirement for success in the global economy.
Many enterprises have achieved significant gains through information automation and global logistics. Indeed, U.S. companies lead the way in this area and in their current productivity advantage in the global marketplace. Frequently, these are described as gains through the systems. Yet, such gains will be short lived if the input/process/output system perspective of the enterprise as a whole is not utilized both by the management and by all

The System Approach as a Strategic Tool in the Global Economy • 127

other stakeholders of the enterprise, employees, suppliers, end use customers, etc.

4. As discussed in Chapters 1 and 2, we are faced with situations where strength in arbitrary combinations among these core competencies was adequate until the recent past. What is needed now is a simultaneous and strategic deployment of all three sets of core competencies at every level: individual, organization, and the enterprise, as illustrated in Figures 6.1 and 6.2. In many respects this would appear to be like solving the puzzle described as Rubik's Cube. The System Approach provides a logical means for this problem. Without such logic, managing of enterprises, organizations, or an individual's career would appear to be as complicated and frustrating as resolving the Rubik's Cube!

Consider, for example, the strategy of a company to achieve sales growth and profitability (technical outputs) through global logistics. The evidences of this may be observed in outsourcing and global purchasing of all kinds (components, subassemblies, engineering functions, etc.). This strategy, in turn, may produce singular improvements of return on investment for shareholders, a system output. The management of the company may or may not deliberately plan for improvements in other system outputs, such as benefits to employees, benefits to supplier industries, etc. The individual employee in such an enterprise with core competence in specialized knowledge of some kind has one of few options when faced with this situation:

- Leave the company to join another where such specialized know-how is needed. This is often stated as the necessary "multiple career changes" that are the product of the era of globalization.
- Accept a lower salary and continue in the present task-oriented position, which is less and less needed.
- Learn the tools of transportation and logistics, and

128 • The System Approach

transfer to a position in the sourcing or purchasing department.

Evidence abounds of this type of career change or career accommodation through information management. Frequently, such career changes are forced upon individuals due to the changes imposed on the enterprise by the global economy. Even when these changes are unintentional, they are perceived as arbitrary and due to poor management. There are too many stories of this nature, and a few of them are referenced in Chapters 1 and 2.

A strategic change process initiated by the enterprise can bring about needed changes in the core competencies of the company and its employees. Today, changes of this nature, initiated by enterprise management, are rare indeed. However, the System Approach allows strategic and synergistic development or change process, both for the enterprise as well as for individual employees.

Alternatively, the employee can take a broad view of his/her employer as an enterprise and establish his/

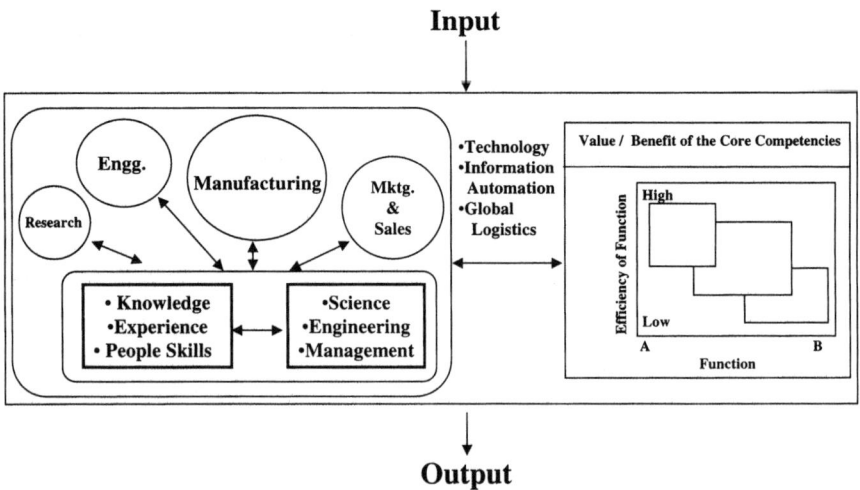

Figure 6.3 • Focus on the common end results—value/benefit of core competencies of the enterprise—leads to a natural alliances between the organizations within an enterprise and among organizations of related industries.

The System Approach as a Strategic Tool in the Global Economy • 129

her own input/process/output system description of the enterprise and its components. (Figure 6.3.) Viewed from the technological point of view, the ultimate or end result of the core competencies can be described within the parameters of meeting certain functional needs of the end-user and the effectiveness or efficiency of their delivery. This analysis helps to identify the core competencies of the enterprise at a given time in terms of technology, information automation, and global logistics. It also helps to identify the appropriate changes needed in the core competencies of the enterprise for long-term success in the global marketplace, taking into account the supplier industries as well as the end-user industries. Then, the employee can assess his/her organization as a system and its core competencies in terms of science, engineering, and management as it presently exists, and also consider the direction for needed changes. Now the employee can assess his/her individual core competencies in terms of knowledge, experience, and people skills, and how they need to be changed, realigned, modified, or enhanced to be in alignment with the needed changes in the core competencies of the organization and the

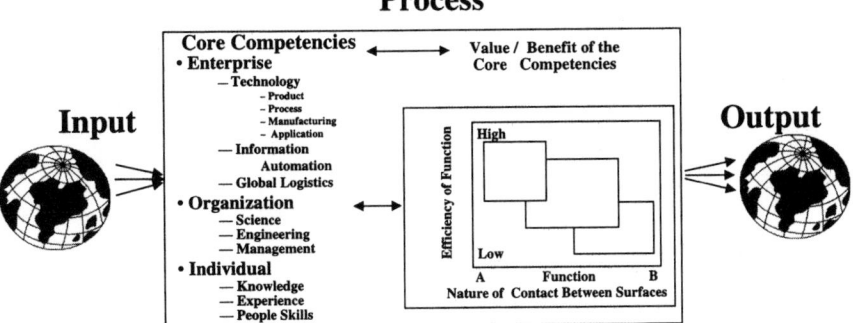

Figure 6.4 • Enterprise as an "input/process/output" transformation engine. The technology in the transformation process determines the value/benefit served. The information automation and global logistics ensure that the input sources are world-wide and the customers served are also on a world-wide basis.

enterprise. These changes are not arbitrary or isolated to the confines of the enterprise. Instead, these changes in core competencies can be seen as needed by viewing the enterprise in the context of its position as a link between the supplier industries and the end use industries on a global basis. (Figure 6.4.) This synergistic deployment of competencies at all levels (individuals, organization, and the enterprise) for a system-oriented enterprise is a cyclic process. (Figure 6.5.) The number of variations and periodicity of this cyclic process has enormously increased thanks to globalization. For those few who recognize this cyclic process, there are boundless opportunities created in the era of global economy.

5. The System Approach is extremely powerful and very much needed for engineering professionals. More frequently than not, engineers are ready to jump into the solution of a problem and look for results that they can measure and relate to (technical outputs). In many

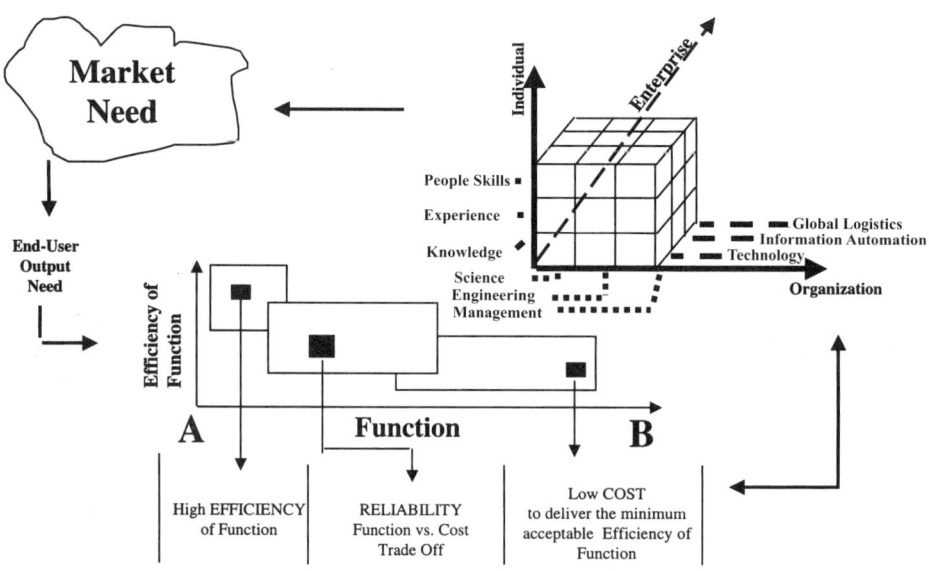

Figure 6.5 • Product/Market segmentation: System Approach permits translation of core competencies into market needs or customer benefits.

instances, engineers treat the system output more as a nuisance or something to be worried about by "managers." The System Approach mandates the viewpoint that system output is the only true output of the industrial activity. In this respect, management is everybody's job. The understanding of the basic scientific principles of the process is also everybody's job. The comprehension of this interdisciplinary thought process is needed for every practicing engineer if he/she is to survive and succeed in the global economy. This need is expressed in many ways through various publications, print media, television reports, etc. The System Approach provides a methodology to be practiced by engineers in every industrial activity to satisfy the needs of the global marketplace.

6. There are serious discussions on the role of basic research versus applied research, science versus engineering, and so on. These types of discussions reinforce our stereotyped view of the world: A) Tasks to be executed individually, B) Sequential tasks and their results that collectively lead to solutions or benefits. C) Such solutions/ benefits are distributed to those involved in the process—investors, managers, employees, etc.—through the organization of tasks and their systematic pursuit. Such segmentation of the problem permits isolation of tasks between basic, applied, science, engineering, management, etc. In the System Approach, such absolute divisions or bifurcation are not recognized.

Even in a task-oriented activity, the reality is much the same. The true measure of the full comprehension of any task is when the person executing the task recognizes its applied or engineering content in addition to the management content of the task, along with the basic or scientific components. When an integrated and interdisciplinary perspective of this type evolves, the individual executing the task transforms from the task execution mind-set to the system-oriented problem resolution mind-set.

The concept and optimization of a system is nothing new for an engineer. Indeed the advancements in industrial society are largely due to development and exploitation of engineering systems of various kinds such as automobiles, ships, planes, missiles, telephones, etc. In a similar fashion, management as a process for effective development and deployment of solutions is also not a new concept for engineers. Engineers have successfully used the organizational tool of project management in every conceivable engineering activity. Over the years, a frame of mind has developed that project management is a distinct and independent activity integrating a large number of engineering activities. Yet, the recent trend is to incorporate project management concepts and software as an integral part of engineering activities. Both of the above observations indicate our present state of task-oriented approaches to problem solving. The need to move away from this task execution mind-set towards the thinking for problem solving appears to be the basic or fundamental need in every aspect of our industrial society. The System Approach provides the means for an interdisciplinary problem solving approach by simultaneously considering the roles of science, engineering, and management components that are necessary to solve any problem.

Thus far we have discussed the role of the System Approach in the context of enterprises and their long-term success, as well as that of individuals and their long-term career development. At this point it will be easy to accept the System Approach as another problem solving methodology, or dismiss it as another management tool. Either of these is perfectly acceptable from an academic point of view. But real life is not simply an academic discussion or a philosophic analysis. The diminishing number of well-paid jobs in a globally competitive enterprise is a reality. The uncertainty of life-long employment in a given enterprise in this era of globalization is also an undeniable reality of our lives. Specialization is now looked upon with disfavor. Specialized knowledge, when replaced, leaves the specialist with little or no safety net in terms of job security. At the same time, generalists with shallow or minimal knowledge can no longer satisfy the needs of a globally competitive marketplace. The higher standard of living in an industrially advanced nation was almost a given, based entirely on place of birth and by assuming that standard available avenues for securing employment opportunities would remain stable. But such higher standards of living, purely based on the place of birth or place of living, are no longer assured in a global economy. Instead, higher standards of living are possible only for those who execute functions whose output and their value to the enterprise exceeds that of anyone else performing similar activities or functions anywhere in the world. This sets the new paradigm for education, job function, and career development. Alternatively, the rewards to justify the effort will merely satisfy the lowest standard of living in any location in the world where the task can be accomplish or executed. In this context the System Approach no longer appears to be a mere academic exercise. Instead, it is the necessary methodology—a process for survival and success in the era of global economy and its associated right-sizing, downsizing, and globalization.

Consider, for example, the following series of questions and answers.

1. What is a job in the global economy?
   The job is defined as participating in an input/process/output system with the objective of achieving quantum improvements in the system output. The input/process/output system is the same for an individual employee and for the enterprise employing him/her.
2. I thought the job was something that I was assigned to by my superior. What happened to these types of jobs?
   A task can be assigned. An input/process/output system cannot be assigned. One simply participates in the system. Your superior participates in the system the same way you participate in the system. In fact, all employees of the enterprise, from the chief executive to the lowest level employee, participate in the same input/

process/output system in a global enterprise.

3. What is the difference between my job and that of my superior?

   Both the employee and the superior participate in the same system. The level of responsibility is determined by the scale or expectation of the system output to be delivered by the employee. Consider profitability as a measure of the system output. This is distinct from profits that, as a measure of the output, are of interest only to those inside the enterprise. Hence, profit is merely a technical output. The relative value of such profits to investors—the return on investment—is of real interest to the investors or those somewhat removed from the day-to-day operations. This means every employee is truly committed to achieve results out of their individual and collective efforts to increase the ROI, which is one of the system outputs. Clearly, the magnitude of impact and direct responsibility on ROI changes from the lowest-level employee to the highest-level executive of the enterprise.

   In addition to the shareholder returns (ROI), there are system outputs of interest to other stakeholders, employees, supplier industries, customer industries, and the enterprise itself. In a global economy, everyone connected with the enterprise at all levels is required to focus on each of these system outputs. In a traditional enterprise, such stakeholder benefits were taken care of by the industry and the society at large. The chief of the enterprise was largely required to focus on the shareholder returns.

   In a global economy, alternatives for impacting stakeholder benefits expand immensely. Also, the ability of individual employees to impact such outputs are greater. As an enterprise transitions into the global economy, constantly increasing the stakeholder benefits—the system outputs—becomes the shared responsibility of the employee and his/her organizational superiors.

4. How can I be assured of job security, when my superior and I participate in the same system as well as my subordinates?
   Job security is no longer the case of retaining an assigned task or switching between available tasks. Instead, job security is the case of preserving and fostering or growing the input/process/output system of the enterprise. In this scenario, the job security of all employees of the enterprise is truly intertwined. In a fundamental sense, everyone sails or everyone sinks with the ship. It is this inevitable linkage of all involved in the enterprise that we have come to recognize as the collective success in a global economy.
5. How can I define the input/process/output system that relates to my job?
   Consider the enterprise you are part of. What are its core competencies in terms of technology, information automation, and global logistics? Next, consider the organization you are part of. What are its core competencies in terms of science, engineering, and management? Finally consider your core competencies at this time in terms of knowledge, experience, and people skills. Now you can describe the input/process/output system for yourself, your organization, and your enterprise, using the models shown in Figures 4.4 and 6.4. The individual's input/process/output system is a subset of the organization, which is a subset of the enterprise viewed as a system.
6. I cannot clearly see the core competencies of my company. What should I do?
   The core competencies of any enterprise are divided among three categories—technology, information automation, and global logistics. Extended discussion of the description of these core competencies was noted in Chapters 3, 4, and 5. Yet, it is neither simple nor easy to perceive all aspects of these three core competencies. But a sustained ability to identify and distinguish these three core competencies of the enterprise renders you,

as an individual, a comprehensive picture of your enterprise and where it is headed in the future as part of the global economy. Besides, identifying the core competence is not an individual effort. Discuss this with your fellow employees, supervisors, suppliers, customers, anyone connected with the system. Identify the basic elements that hold all of these people together. The core competencies become identified as part of this interactive analysis of who we are, what are we striving for, why, and how.

7. What should be the right balance between the three core competencies for my enterprise?

    The answer to this question depends on the level of responsibility you have in the system. The answer to this question is most critical for the chief of the enterprise. Indeed, this desired balance between the core competencies of technology, information automation, and global logistics sets the strategy of the enterprise in the global economy.

    On the other hand, the lower your level in the organization, the more your need to recognize the existing balance between these three core competencies and how the balance is being shifted as part of globalization. The balance between recognition of core competencies versus initiation of actions to change or rebalance the core competencies shifts as the employee's job function and responsibility in the enterprise increases. In the System Approach, this shift will be gradual rather than discrete.

8. I would like to influence the core competencies of my organization and the enterprise. What should I do?

    The core competencies of any organization are science, engineering, and management. Your individual competencies of knowledge, experiences, and people skills are directly linked to these three core competencies. Your individual ability and the needs of your organization are matched when all three of your individual core competencies are simultaneously deployed to strengthen the three core competencies of the organization. This 3x3 matrix may not be perfectly balanced with equal weight in each of the nine cells. Indeed there will be a constant need to shift the deployment among the three individual core competencies in order to meet the shifts in the balance among the three core competencies of the organization. It is by the ability to gain new or additional strengths among each of the three individual core competencies, as needed, and then deploying them to meet the changing scenarios of the core competencies of the organization that allows an employee to influence the long-term survival and success of the organization. This in turn is the key for long-term success of individual employees in an enterprise.

The true comprehension of the core competencies is a necessary asset for every individual in the global economy. We have dealt with the core competence of technology in some detail in Chapter 4. We have also described the aspects of core competencies such as automation and logistics in Chapter 5. But we need a clear comprehension of information automation and global logistics, as these are the two of the three competencies of any enterprise.

In its broad context, information automation represents the ability to generate, collect, analyze, and disseminate knowledge and information with the highest level of efficiency in terms of cost, time, utility, etc. This is a broad and comprehensive ability that is much larger in scope and impact than the practices of data processing and information processing would imply. For instance, an automated worldwide database is merely a technical tool. But when the database becomes a tool for the larger cross section of the enterprise to make decisions effectively and efficiently, the enterprise would be considered successful in its core competence of information automation. This analogy should be extended to every aspect of knowledge in the enterprise to visualize the full impact and meaning of information automation as a core competence. It is the effective deployment of this core competence which is frequently referred to as "Information Technology," "Information Age," "Information Society," "Digital Economy," etc.

Global logistics, as a core competence of the enterprise, needs to be understood in its entirely as well. Global logistics translates far beyond the mere technical processes of moving information, people, objects, or cash around the world. Sometimes it is described as the global mind, which represents a mind-set to think in terms of worldwide opportunities. In its entirety, global logistics refers to the recognition of the entire world as a source for all the needed inputs, or resources, as well as the beneficiary of the end product of the input/process/output system. This description of global logistics is illustrated in Figures 2.4 and 2.5. The "rapid growth in service industry" is a frequently used phrase to refer to the effect of global logistics in our society. A true comprehension of global logistics is impossible within the context of our task-oriented approach for problem-solving. For instance, sourcing of raw materials, sourcing of finished goods, transfer of people across geographies, setting up plants in various corners of the world, investment of cash in various regions of the world, etc., would come to mind as representations of global logistics. Yet, these are mere listings of technical outputs, where global logistics plays a role as a core competency. The personal knowledge and experience of every employee of the enterprise on a worldwide basis, their cultures, and their aspirations can lead to unprecedented growth opportunities for the enterprise, especially when it is skillfully combined (global logistics) with the other core competencies of technology and information automation. Similarly, an organization within the enterprise may find worldwide opportunities for its core competencies of science, engineering, and management by careful assessment and deployment of global logistics. An individual employee can enhance the effectiveness of his/her core competencies of knowledge/experience/people skills on a worldwide basis by seeking out opportunities to deploy them through appropriate core competencies of the organization and the enterprise. Indeed, these are all the untapped opportunities, now made accessible through the tools of information technology, communications technology, and transportation technology. These are the engines driving the core competence of global logistics.

9. Why do the core competencies of my organization change?

An enterprise, in order to survive and succeed in a global economy, needs to deploy appropriate balance between its core competencies of technology, information automation, and global logistics. The shift and rebalance among these core competencies is achieved by changing the core competencies of the organization. In order to cope with these changes, individuals have to rebalance their core competencies among knowledge, experience, and people skills. This constant juggling act appears random and haphazard if viewed from individual instances and numerous statistical metrics. On the other hand, these changes are easy to perceive, maneuver, and steer if they are viewed as an integral part of the input/process/output, system at the enterprise, organizational, and individual levels.

10. I understand the three core competencies at each level—enterprise, organization, and myself as an individual. What is next?

Once the core competencies are perceived, one can begin to investigate what leads to these core competencies. Core competencies do not occur arbitrarily. We can recognize that they are driven or caused by the simultaneous influence of four input groups. In turn, the core competencies manifest as outputs, classified between technical or internal outputs and external or system outputs.

The four input groups have their distinct features. One of them is associated with the availability of wealth or capital resources. The second is associated with consumable resources, which can be deployed in desired quantities. The third input always deals with the "product," or intended end use or application. The fourth has to do with the factors (or operating environment) under which the above three input groups are brought together.

The need for changes in core competencies are influenced by the need for changes in the system output. The changing needs in the system output can be met by changing one input group at a time. But the largest impact is achieved when all four input groups are modulated simultaneously.

This procedure and practice, the System Approach, is the same for individuals, organizations, and the enterprise as a whole. At every level, the objective is to serve as a resource to solve a problem or meet the desired system outputs.

Problem solvers are capable of:
- (a) Developing the description of the input/process/output system at the appropriate level—individual, organization, or enterprise.
- (b) Defining the problem in terms of needed quantum changes in the system output at the appropriate level.
- (c) Translating these systems output goals into technical outputs, based on external causal relations.
- (d) Identifying pertinent internal causal relations and their measurements, and how they reflect or represent the technical outputs.
- (e) Identifying the needed changes in the internal causal relationships and the needed changes in the core competencies at the appropriate level.
- (f) Accomplishing the needed changes in all four input groupings simultaneously, thereby achieving the needed changes in the core competencies.

The System Approach as a Strategic Tool in the Global Economy • 141

(g) Recognizing that changes in core competencies can be verified through appropriate process measures.
(h) Affecting the desired changes in core competencies that lead to the desired technical outputs, which in turn are linked to the desired changes in the system output.
(i) Recognizing the system outputs as the representations of the value/benefit of the input/process/output system.

Thus, the System Approach has the power to transform an individual from a narrow focused, task-oriented worker to an interdisciplinary, team-oriented creator or developer of value/benefits. Such a person is described as project oriented, entrepreneurial, results oriented, flexible, adaptive, etc. These are the natural attributes inherent to the System Approach.

For such a system-oriented problem solver, knowledge, experience, and people skills are the core competencies to be developed and deployed simultaneously. Thus, performance of the job in terms of problem-solving is both a learning process and a process for deployment of the learning for achieving quantum improvements in the system outputs. In this context, life long learning, often cited as a requirement for survival in the global economy, becomes relevant and meaningful.

The system-oriented problem solver recognizes the science, engineering, and management context in every problem. Such a problem solver gains insights to these three cores needs and deploys them adequately and directly through his/her personal knowledge or experience, or from others through his/her people skills. These competencies needed for problem-solving are constantly matched with the needed core competencies of the enterprise under which the problem is being solved. Hence, parallel processing and multi-tasking are not merely an optional way of deploying core competencies. They are the only way.

The System Approach would appear to be a powerful tool for development and long-term success of the enterprise, as well as its employees and all other stakeholders. One might wonder why such an approach, seemingly powerful and valuable, has not found widespread use. This would be particularly intriguing in light of all the expressed needs to survive and succeed in the global economy. Many if not all of these needs would appear to be met as a natural outcome of the System Approach. We shall explore some of the reasons limiting the wide spread use of this methodology in the following pages. By no means are these intended to be absolute or final. Instead, it is hoped that such analysis will lead to further discussion, and to actions that are necessary for the future.

The first and foremost impediment to the System Approach is our mindset. As has been repeated many times earlier, the success of the industrial societies has been through the dissection of problems into small enough segments to allow each segment to represent one or a few specific tasks. Organized collections of the tasks can then represent a problem.

From a historical perspective, individuals have evolved with specific mind-sets to fathom the details of a problem. These individuals were called scientists and scholars. Later on, such detailed study on any and all facets of the problem became possible through unprecedented levels of specialization. Such pursuit of the details has been described as research work. Thus, scientific studies in the early part of the 20th century were followed by research studies of all kinds in the middle and later part of the century. Similarly, the application of this specialized knowledge to conceive, design, and build products and services of value came into vogue. These have been described as engineering activities. To facilitate such engineering activities, people with expertise in specific technical tasks were developed. This type of knowledge was supplemented with people trained in vocational education. Ultimately, people with or without formal and specialized education were trained to carry out individual tasks. We have come to call them blue-collar workers.

With the preponderance of individuals possessing the ability to carry out assigned tasks, it became necessary to identify, organize, and coordinate all these tasks to achieve the desired end results. As this need was being fulfilled, the "science of management" was born. It should surprise no one that schools of management became fully established and gained prominence only in the middle to later half of the 20th century. This dissection of the problem into tasks and their coordinated execution through "management" has systemized a vast majority of industrial activities. Along with that has come an unprecedented level of efficiency in the execution of tasks and their collective benefit—called productivity—enjoyed by the industrial societies.

Now, we stand at the threshold of a new paradigm. A large majority of the tasks carried out by individuals, in terms of information collection, processing, and dissemination, can be efficiently handled through tools of information automation. (Figure 2.4.) In addition, the global economy permits us to utilize and integrate resources and workers from any part of the world. Being born in an industrially advanced nation no longer gives preference or privilege to an individual in terms of the availability of task-oriented jobs. The lowest standard of living (and hence the lowest cost of labor) available anywhere in the world becomes the prevailing standard for executing any task-oriented activity. These descriptions are not intended to arouse economic class wars or passions of that nature. On the contrary, these conclusions are the result of the summary of evidences, which are collectively described as globalization. These are the logical and inevitable consequences of advancements in technology and competencies pertaining to information automation and global logistics.

The natural outcome of the above is a simple conclusion. Anyone, anywhere in the world, can achieve and maintain the highest standard of living, provided the output of his/her efforts are better than anyone else anywhere in the world. This is the rule of global economy. In order to achieve such world-class excellence, it will be necessary for everyone to be able to define and describe the overall benefit or value of his/her activity (the system output), and describe the input/process/

output system that defines or describes such activity. This methodology or outlook and its effective use to achieve world-class performance in terms of quantum increase in the system output is the System Approach.

This transition from a mind-set of task execution to the mind-set of systems thinking will be the single biggest challenge faced by all of us in every facet of our life. The chief of an enterprise can successfully lead the enterprise through globalization, with benefits to all stakeholders. On the contrary, the enterprise could set specific task-oriented or technical output goals, only to find out that even after meeting such goals the enterprise becomes an entity being lost in global economic pressures. All professionals—scientists, engineers, and managers—will be increasingly required to merge their specialized areas into an interdisciplinary process with an eye on solving the problem. In this process the clear lines of distinction between blue-collar, white-collar, supervisory, and management functions will be blurred. Distinctions will be based more on the amount of responsibility for the scale of the system, and the value of the system for the society. At every level of the system, the individuals, organizations, or the enterprise will be required at the minimum to be aware of the input/process/output system of which they are a part. Beyond this recognition, the progression moves to the next stage of strategic deployment, through the appropriate use of internal and external causal relations. We shall call this stage of progress the "analysis" capability of the input/process/output systems. The progression then moves to the stage of identifying predetermined stakeholder benefits (system outputs), and rendering them a reality through synthesis of novel input/process/output systems. This transition in job functions or performance is illustrated in Figure 6.6.

The second impediment to our pursuit of the System Approach is the resistance to change. Despite all of the evidence pointing to the need to shift away from task-oriented functioning of individuals and organizations, it is difficult to accept the shift after years of status quo. In many instances

The System Approach as a Strategic Tool in the Global Economy • 145

it requires a forced habit to look beyond the traditional approaches. Often, incremental benefits from traditional practices render the shift to the new paradigm as something that can be postponed until another day.

The third, and perhaps more important, impediment to the pursuit of the System Approach is a need for collective change. Consider for example an employee in the industrial enterprise. He/she perceives the larger purpose of the job function or the system and effectively participates in it by cutting across traditional organizational boundaries. The productivity and effectiveness of the employee is huge. Yet, the employee and his/her outputs will be of significant impact only if there is a synergistic pursuit of the System Approach by everyone else around him/her—peers, superiors, and subordinates. Absent such collective change, the individual, despite the best of intentions, will be caught in the conflict between task-oriented problem solving versus the system-oriented problem resolution. This is illustrated in Figure 6.7.

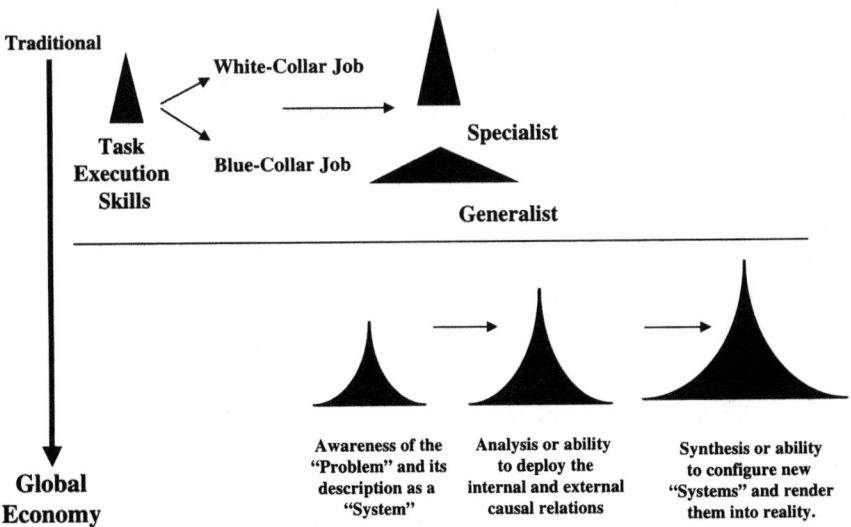

Figure 6.6 • *Knowledge development: task-oriented vs. system-oriented.*

146 • The System Approach

The System Approach permits the development of entrepreneurial Problem Solving approach to Job Functions. In this regard it creates conflicts with the task focussed job functions.

The System Approach finds a natural fit to accommodate the needed changes in job functions when task oriented jobs are eliminated during the process of Globalization.

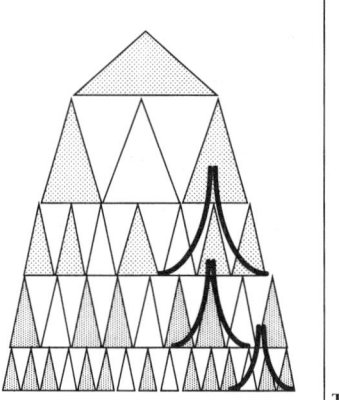
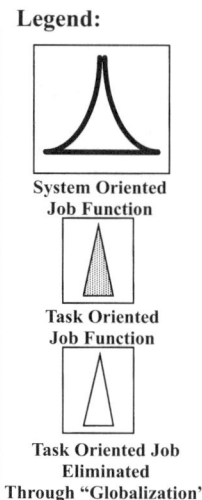

Figure 6.7 • *Need for enterprise-wide changes for the most effective implementation of the System Approach.*

The need for collective change extends beyond individual employees of the enterprise. Consider current accounting practices as an example. The tools of measurement—often called accounting practices—were developed to manage task-oriented activities. For example, costs associated with manufacture, sales and marketing, engineering/research/development, and administration are tracked independently in large enterprises. Each department is held responsible for its functions and the associated costs. In contrast, in an entrepreneurial effort of solving a problem, one or more individuals may cut across several functions from market research, concept development, research, engineering, manufacturing, sales, and overall performance and profitability assessment. There is a great deal of flexibility and latitude in an entrepreneurial system in tracking of costs, as long as the overall goals are achieved.

The larger the enterprise, the more it moves away from the flexible, entrepreneurial processes to more task-oriented structures. This is often necessary in order to be amenable to established procedures and practices. For large enterprises to perform and function as a system-oriented entrepreneurial team will require methods of measurement, accounting practices for example, that embrace the System Approach. Similar conclusions can also be made for human resources management. The measures of responsibility and reward that are traditionally linked to a specific task need to be changed. The change will be needed to reflect the responsibility for the results or problem resolution, rather than on the size or scale of the task managed. In such a classification process, responsibility for interdisciplinary thinking, problem definition in terms of stakeholder benefits, and problem resolution in terms of system output, will be recognized and rewarded. This needed transformation in the assessment of value/benefit of the job functions is another impediment to the pursuit of the System Approach.

But the need for collective change should not become a deterrent for individuals. On the contrary, the adoption of the System Approach is the only way for individuals and organizations to survive and succeed in the era of globalization, and its associated down-sizing and right-sizing. As we have discussed earlier, the System Approach is a methodology for development and deployment of critical core competencies at every level—from individual, to organization, to enterprise. Manipulating these core competencies, by simultaneous change in the four input groups, leads to quantum changes in the system output. Thus, recognizing the change process from the task-oriented job function to system-oriented problem resolution is part of the deployment of the core competence. To the extent there is an enterprise wide change to adopt the System Approach, the organization and the individuals embracing it will find their transition as necessary and welcome. Absent such enterprise wide transition, the organization and individuals have a need to become the catalysts in the change process for the long-term success of the enterprise.

We have discussed the need for collective change within an organization or enterprise. But the need for collective change extends beyond such industrial organizations and entities. What does a global enterprise truly represent in terms of national economics, employment level, and standards of living within an individual country? These and other related issues are beyond the scope of this book. We shall consider here only one aspect of the societal issues, education, within the context of the System Approach.

As we have discussed earlier, education—one of the key sources of knowledge building for individuals—needs to be viewed in a fundamentally different manner as we move from a task-oriented society to a process-oriented or systems thinking society. We have evidence for such a need in every facet of our educational systems. The college accreditation procedure is being reviewed. Every school system is looking into improving and upgrading their education processes to achieve world-class standards. Yet, after some reference to the identification of such a need, we seem to immediately jump to task-oriented problem-solving. Curriculum review, testing of school teachers, increased school hours, computers for every student, more homework, advanced placement courses, tax credit for tuition fees, and smaller class sizes are among the popular solutions. Taken individually, these efforts will only lead to incremental improvements or no measurable change at all. This may be an unpopular conclusion.

Are there educational processes at colleges for the teachers that can prepare them to educate students for the global economy? Is there a need for a fundamental transition in our educational processes at all levels, or is it merely a case of better education in our elementary, middle, and high schools? What is life-long education, often referred to as a need in the global economy? How does the education process prepare one for life long learning? Leaders of the society have a role to initiate, foster, and synthesize comprehensive answers to the above questions. This, in turn, will lead to an input/process/output system description of the educational process at all levels—from elementary school to the highest levels. Such transition from task-oriented to system-oriented education at all levels, permitting the transition described in Figure 6.6, may be the single greatest need in every industrial society as we enter the 21st century.

Chapter 7
Personal Concerns and the System Approach

Mark Reardon—The Enterprise Manager

Mark Reardon was standing near the large window in his corner office, watching a bird perched on the treetop outside. It was an adult robin, identical in appearance to another robin that Mark and his wife had saved after finding it on the ground during a storm. He had fed the bird and kept it warm, even though he had little hope for its survival. But, to his surprise, it grew and seemed very content in its nesting box. While raising the bird, Mark felt affection and a bond for the rapidly growing, but vulnerable, creature. Then, suddenly one day without notice, it just flew away.

But Mark was not really thinking about the bird. It was a metaphor of his thoughts. The bird was the company that he had presided over as president for the past six years. The company seemed to have escaped and flown away, out of his control. Mark had risen from the ranks and had made his division one of the most profitable and successful operations in the company. His accomplishments were rewarded. He rose gradually higher up in the organization ladder. Last week, when he was invited to the corporate headquarters, he had hoped for greater challenges. Instead, he was advised that his division had been sold to a group of investors from Namibia. The investors had made an offer that the board could not reject in clear conscience, keeping the shareholders best interest in mind. "Where did I go wrong?" was the question constantly reverberating in his mind.

Mark had never been away from his small town in the Mid-West, except for occasional corporate meetings in Chicago, about 200 miles away. Now, the prospect of having to deal with new owners from a far corner of the globe daunted him. What should he do? How should he handle this new situation? Is this merely the tip of the iceberg? His thoughts and questions seemed endless.

• • •

It was well past sunset, and the darkness of the night was slowly creeping in. The tree he was viewing was barely visible, and there was no longer a bird to be seen on the treetop. Nevertheless, Mark was unconcerned about what he could not see in the expanding darkness. Instead, his mind was racing at full speed as he began to see more clearly and visibly the situation as it was unfolding.

He recalled the recent conversation at headquarters, after he had been informed that the operation that he is heading up as the president had just been sold to the group of investors. He decided to review the situation again, one step at a time. Why investors from Namibia? "Why not?" Mark concluded. Investment is a form of input of capital or fixed assets into an enterprise. Return on investment is the system output sought after by investors. Mark knew that the ROI of his operation had been consistently around 5 to 7% for the past fifteen years. He had been proud of this accomplishment. "We have never been in the red; we have been highly dependable in our performance; we have never fluctuated wildly in ROI," Mark said repeatedly to his bankers and other financial analysts. Now, with his objective analysis, Mark realized that his personal assets have been growing at 10 to 12% in equity investments. "Hold it. If I can make better returns elsewhere, I wouldn't be investing in a 5 to 7% ROI operation. No wonder our investors have decided to walk away from our business," Mark concluded.

Mark returned to the question: "Why investors from Namibia?" Well, his personal investments included diversified portfolios. He used this strategy to help protect personal assets, while accommodating fluctuations in the global marketplace.

Today more than ever, it is possible to invest anywhere in the world, thanks to globalization. Modern information systems permit us to manage our investments on a twenty-four hour basis. Moving them across various locations from the four corners of the globe is also easier than ever. We call this "information automation." Indeed, Mark had been under pressure to look for resources anywhere in the world. Mark had resisted this pressure, and now it appeared that he had been fighting the wrong battle. Perhaps the Namibian investors had actually been identified and attracted by the financial institution that served his company's international customers. "So this is what global logistics is all about," reflected Mark.

Mark's thoughts began to race beyond the investors from Namibia. It was clear that "information automation" and "global logistics" were two forces influencing his enterprise. "What else?" Mark asked next. In search of answers to this question, Mark started asking other people in the company, "What is our business?"

At first, this seemed like a strange question to many of his employees. "Mark, you know what we do. Do you have any doubts about it?" was the most frequent response. It was also a challenge for Mark to control the rumor mill and put down the apprehensions raised by this simple question: "What is our business?" Finally, the feedback started pouring in. Much of it reflected each department's operational role, as each responded to the question as it related to their primary functions. Research, for example, reported that their business was new product development, and Manufacturing reported that their business was making products at the right quality, quantity, cost, and timeliness. The Sales organization reported that their business was getting the products to the customers, thus achieving sales.

Mark persisted. He wanted a single description of the overall business. The more he insisted on this, the more he received a diversity of responses. Research further defined their response, describing the business in terms of incremental products and breakthrough products. Manufacturing refined their description in terms of made items versus stock items. Marketing described it in terms of loss leaders, cash cows, and bread and butter large volume business. Sales described the business in terms of sales regions, market segments, distribution systems, and direct customers.

"Enough is enough," said Mark. "We can't have so many descriptions of our business," he decided. "We need to get out of the box. We're looking at our business from our limited points of view and as perceived by each of our organizations. Let's step back as far as we can and look at why our customers buy our products, and also why they buy those of our competitors. There must be some common reason why our customers need all these products."

Mark Reardon's company is a manufacturer of mechanical components that can be broadly grouped under the heading of bearings, gears, and slides. Each of these product lines has unique functions, end-uses, and methods of manufacture. The customers were buying these products, as well as those of their competitors, to be assembled in their equipment in the form of subassemblies and assemblies. The parts function in diverse ways, from small mechanical appliances and toys, to industrial equipment such as machine tools. A wide variety of these products were also used in automo-

Personal Concerns and the System Approach • 153

biles, aircraft engines, ships, and other marine applications. Recently, in an effort to expand into the high tech industry, some product lines had been added, such as bearing, slides, and shafts used in both printers and copiers.

Despite the diversity of products, markets, and applications, Mark began to see common themes. Viewed from a very large perspective, the products seemed to serve two functions. In almost every situation Mark's products were used to achieve relative motion between contacting surfaces. In addition, every situation required a measure of the function or the efficiency in achieving this relative motion between the contacting surfaces. Invariably, the customers needed to achieve a balance between the nature of contact and the efficiency of function between the contacting surfaces. "This is the end effect or value/benefit of all our competencies at every level," concluded Mark. (Figure 7.1.)

Now Mark's creative juices started flowing. The more he thought about it, the more clear it all became. All the diverse

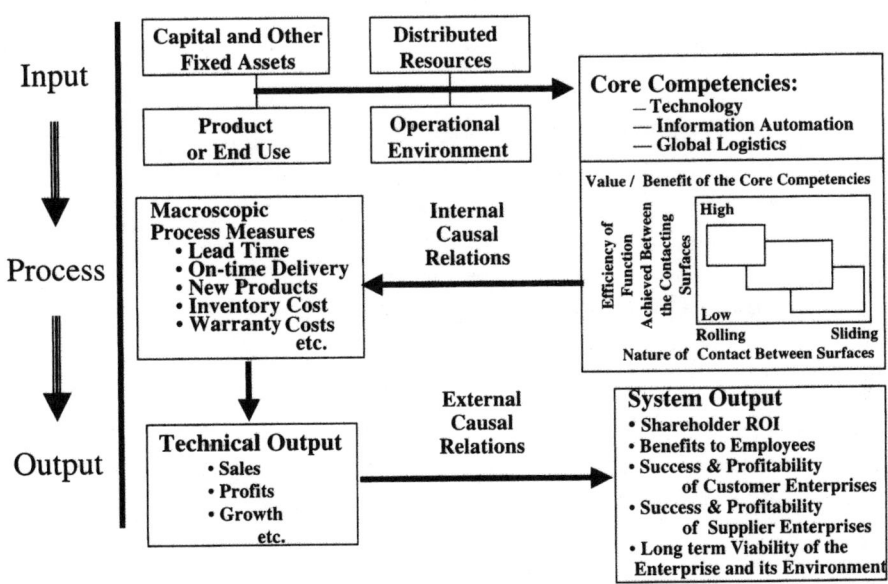

Figure 7.1 • *Mark Reardon's enterprise represented as an input/process/output system.*

154 • The System Approach

descriptions of his business began to gel into a single picture. It was no longer a case of fitting the jigsaw puzzle between Research, Development, Manufacturing, and Marketing, etc. Instead, there was a seamless connection—cause and effect—between the activities of the various organizations and the end-result of the enterprise (Figure 7.2).

"The purpose of my enterprise is to help my customers achieve the desired efficiency of function while achieving the desired nature of contact between the surfaces of their components," concluded Mark. "To this end, we have technologies to configure the desired contacting surfaces or function of the components (Product Technology). We have know-how to reduce this configuration into objects (Process Technology). We have the know-how for the repeated use of the process technologies to achieve products as needed by our customers in terms of quantity, place, and time (Manufacturing Technology)." Mark's thoughts moved toward the conclusion that the cost and quality seemed to be merely the boundary conditions

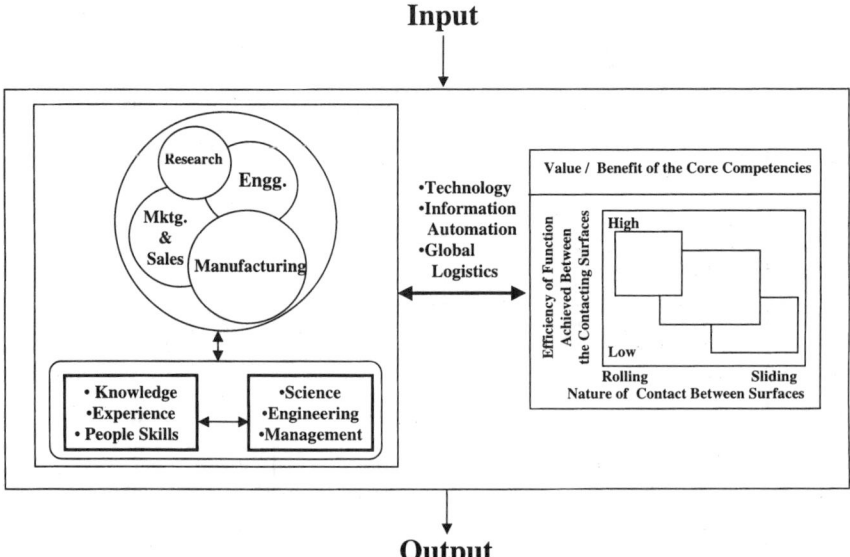

Figure 7.2 • Through the focus on integrated deployment of core competencies at every level, the organizations of Mark Reardon's enterprise became well integrated parts of an input/process/output system.

in meeting the quantity, place, and time needs of the customers along with the intended value/benefits. Finally, he noted that the company has strengths in the knowledge or know-how about the use or application of the products by its customers (Applications Technology).

Mark was beginning to feel more and more comfortable with the assessment of the technology as a core competency of his enterprise. He could see the interconnections between the technology in terms of products, processes, manufacturing, and applications. It was beginning to dawn on Mark that these core competencies in technology were to be observed in all parts of his enterprise. Anyone connected with his company—employees, suppliers, users, etc.—were affected by these versions of technology as their core competency. Every aspect of improvement in the functions of the company, such as research and development, product management, manufacturing, marketing, and sales, became one aspect or another

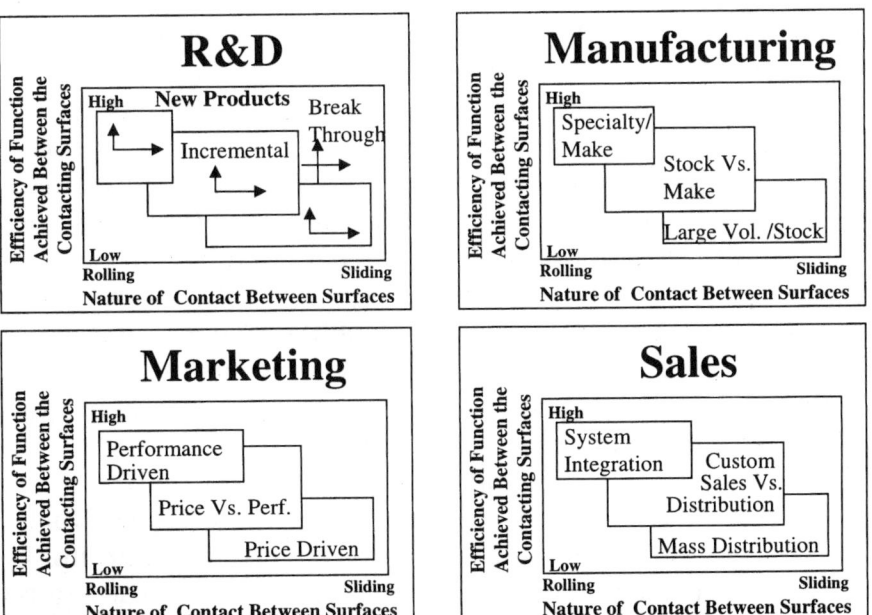

Figure 7.3 • Value/benefit of Mark Reardon's enterprise viewed from its organizations and their perspectives.

for delivering this core competency through the value/benefit scheme in the desired balance (Figure 7.3).

Viewed from this perspective, the need for this value/benefit as the result of the core competency had existed forever. "This has been the reason for the stability in our industry," concluded Mark. If there were to be means to transfer motion between surfaces without contact, then it will result in a new paradigm. Mark could not envision such a radical new technology, but he decided to keep an eye out for such radical changes, as they were the real competitive technological threats to his industry.

"What else has changed in the past decade?" wondered Mark. Every organization in the company contained an administrative component. This was true for research, procurement, purchasing, marketing, manufacturing, human resources, accounting, etc. In every one of these function's administration, its ultimate purpose seemed to be those activities involved in collection, processing, and dissemination of information. In many instances, even analysis of the information was frequently standardized.

In the past decade or so, all these aspects of information could be automated. The process started with management of information. Frequently, this information management was necessary to meet the requests from headquarters. "No wonder. We started our MIS (Management Information Systems) department about 12 years ago," reflected Mark. "Now they are into everything—payroll, benefits management, sales reporting, operations, customer service, purchasing, accounts, etc. Didn't I recently hear the research and development guys talking about a database with the MIS department?"

This sequence of reflections resulted in Mark realizing that "The old MIS department has progressively changed to IM (Information Management), to Computer Systems, and finally to the Information Technology department. But, they don't create any product, process, manufacturing, or applications. Instead, they help each of these technology components of the company and their associated organizations to collect, analyze, report, and utilize information effectively. In all these, the IT department has seemed to automate these processes of information management. Perhaps it is more appropriate to conclude that information automation is a core competency that permeates my company in any and all of its activities," concluded Mark.

The benefits of information automation were readily apparent to Mark. He could not have maintained the 5 to 7% ROI yearly without help from information automation, which had increased the productivity of all his organizations. "Productivity increases usually meant getting the job done with fewer people. Instead, if we would have done more with information automation and our output had expanded, perhaps we could have achieved 8 to 10% ROI. Then I could have retained many of our long-term employees while meeting investor expectations of 5 to 7% ROI." This possibility intrigued Mark, as he remembered, with great deal of sorrow, several of his workers whom he had to let go. "Perhaps I could have shown greater vision and leadership, instead of blindly following a predetermined set of numbers (in terms of profits and ROI) as my only goal," reflected Mark. The distinctions between the technical and system output of his job began to come clear to him.

"How could I have accomplished greater output of my enterprise, while maintaining the many projects already in the works?" wondered Mark. He was determined to find a way. The first thing that came to his mind was the sales orders he had turned down a few months ago. These were for products at a price he could never satisfy. Overseas competition, mostly from the economically emerging nations, was killing him. He knew those customers well. He could understand their need for price reduction and, hence, using products from overseas sources. Well, Mark himself had told his purchasing department to lower costs in any way they can. "Could I source these products from the overseas manufacturers and supply to my customers?" wondered Mark. "After all, we produced these items for many years. We don't make them any more, as they are becoming commodity items with lower margins. But we have the customer contacts, distribution networks, and applications know-how. We have the information automation skills that can make these products flow through our operations, so that it is of no special concern to our customers. Could I have increased my sales by 5% with a marginal cost increase, and added some dollars to my bottom line? Perhaps I could have used this marginal increase in profits for developing new opportunities for my company," he concluded.

• • •

The next day, Mark convened the key individuals from all of his departments and said to them, "I want to increase sales by 5%. I would like to look at low cost products from one of the Far East countries. What limits us from doing that?"

The response came fast and furious: "It will cost us too much. It will not be profitable. Our competitors have low overheads. Their after sales service is poor. Our customers expect more than products from us, etc." The feedback seemed endless. Everyone seemed to be right. Yet, no one seemed to look at his job beyond his small vantage point. Mark was determined to change this paradigm of task oriented job functions.

"We buy raw materials from our suppliers. Do we have any suppliers in these Far East countries?" asked Mark. "Yes, we do. We have 6.32% of our raw materials and blank stock purchase originating from these countries. These have helped us lower our raw material cost by 3.81% each year for the last four years," replied the Purchasing Manager, as he smiled at the Information Systems manager. He could not have been so precise and fast in his response, except for the new IT tools implemented in his department.

"So we do get raw materials from various parts of the world, transform them into products, and sell them to our customers," commented Mark as he considered the information. This seemed obvious to everyone. "But what we are missing is a company-wide mind-set and capability that will allow us to transfer items—raw materials, components, finished goods, knowledge, ideas, or anything of benefit to us—that will help our customers to transmit relative motion between contacting surfaces and achieve the desired efficiency of function in this process," he concluded. Everyone in the room immediately understood. No one could believe that they had not seen this before. Mark slowly repeated the above sentence, so that all could hear it clearly.

The Purchasing Manager for the first time realized that he was part of a "transfer" function. The R&D Manager for the first time heard Mark use the phrases "contacting surfaces" and "efficiency of function of the contacting surfaces." For many participants, the discussion that followed was most enlightening they had ever taken part in. As a result, the term global logistics became more and more clear to everyone. By the end of the week Mark had everyone thinking of their jobs as parts of an interconnected web influenced by three core competencies—technology, information automation, and global logistics. This was the beginning of a long-term transformation of the entire company.

The boundaries between departments and organizations slowly vanished. Instead, there were people who had expertise in one of the three core competencies in all organizations with a clear knowledge of the other two. The growing use of information automation brought unprecedented increases in the efficiency of operations. Meetings, which used to take hours, now ended in minutes, as everyone was focused on solving the same problem. The word "meeting" in itself slowly vanished from the vocabulary and was replaced by information transfer activity. "We are all part of the same system," was the frequently heard comment through out the company. The "system" they referred to was clear in everyone's perception, as well as in all their activities (Figure 7.1).

• • •

Several years have passed since the acquisition of Mark Reardon's company by the investors from Namibia. Since then, the company has changed hands many times. Things were not always easy or peaceful, far from it. The company, however, had survived many ups and downs in the marketplace. Acquisitions, mergers, start ups of new competitors, and spin-offs of new companies were all part of the customer scenario. Despite the turbulence, Mark Reardon had transformed his company into an agile, flexible, responsive, and stable worldwide company. Their suppliers, customers, and competitors constantly recruited his employees. Yet, not many left. Most were happy to be part of an entrepreneurial company that posed few organizational barriers (Figure 7.2). The company had transformed itself into a worldwide organization with clearly identified common value benefits to the end customers (Figure 7.3). Their network of operations at all levels—R&D, Advanced Engineering, Manufacturing, Sales and Customer Service—were worldwide, operating on a 24 hour a day basis. The customers could never fathom if they were dealing with a large company or small one. Information automation and global logistics permitted the company to present any version of the product to the customer as needs changed. The company could meet large volume orders and service them with the same ease and efficiency as they could for small, niche markets worldwide (Figure 7.4). The technology of the company was a constant engine churning out solutions to customer needs, large or small.

It was hard for the customer to recognize if they were relying on Mark's enterprise for their products, process, manufacturing, or applications technology. At times it was even harder to separate the developments in customer solutions from their source. Was it technology, information automation, or global logistics? Indeed, they had begun to consider Mark's company more as an extension of their own company, rather than an external entity. It was not uncommon for Mark's engineers and sales staff to be treated as part of the customer's internal teams. Mark had read in several articles on globalization that a "seamless" connection with the customers is needed to succeed in the global economy. Much to Mark's delight, such

Personal Concerns and the System Approach • 161

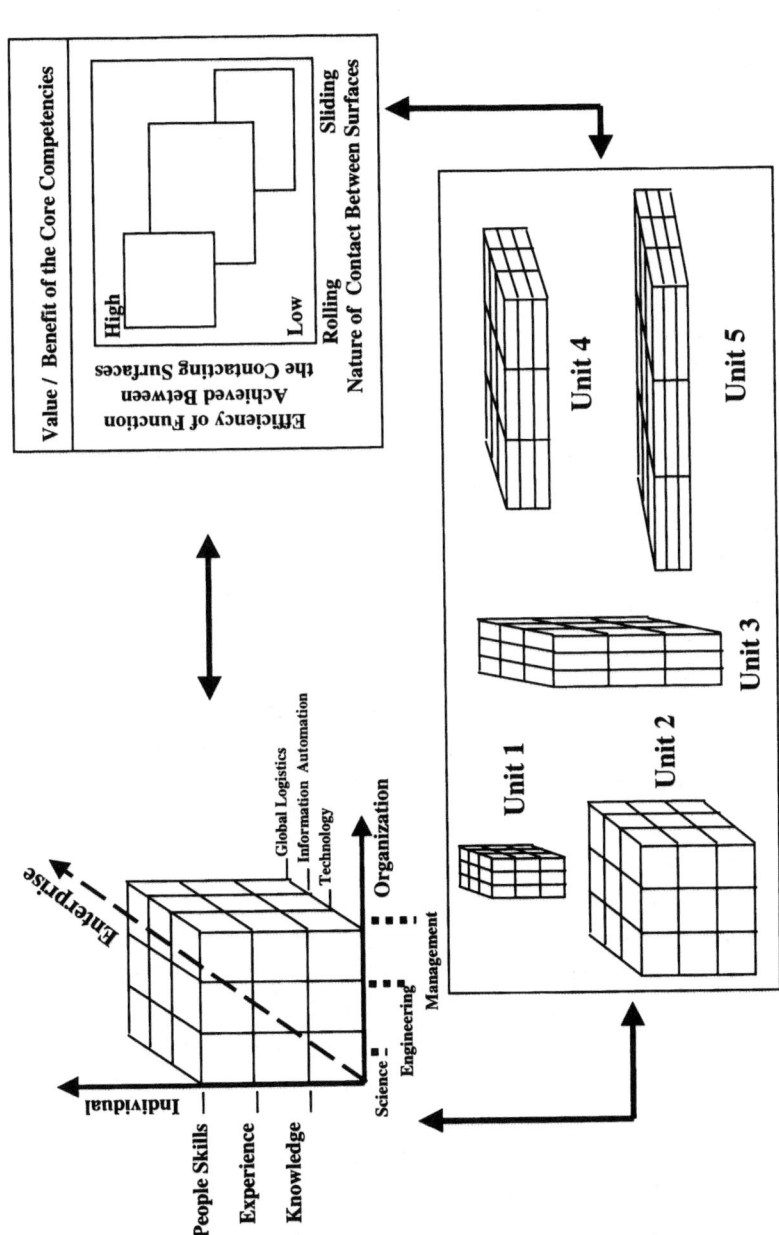

Figure 7.4 • Integrated deployment of core competencies results in the effective responsiveness of the enterprise to meet multiple or niche market needs in the global economy, yet based on common value/benefits (or technology platforms).

seamless connections were happening in his enterprise. After all everyone in Mark's company was looking beyond their own company. They were collectively looking out for the success of their customer companies as one of the system outputs.

Steve Wong–Professional Engineer

Steve Wong could not believe his eyes. He had not left his home for several days, despite the best urging from his wife and family members. Everyone told him that what he was going through was normal. "It is more fashionable to be laid off these days," joked one of his friends. Finally, he had gathered courage to look beyond his books and folders. He started reading some general publications. The first article he read stunned him. There could be no better description of his personal situation. Here is what he read.[16]

> *I was downsized at 9:30 a.m. on Monday, April 3, 1995. I'll never forget the time and date. I was born at that precise moment 32 years earlier. As Dave Barry likes to say, "I'm not making this up." The company that recruited me with much fanfare just a year before pulled out the trick candles on my birthday and gave me a separation package as a present.*
>
> *When I pointed out the company's poor timing to the human resources director as we sat in her office stumbling through my walking papers, she seemed surprised: "Really? I'm so sorry!"*
>
> *After the company disbanded my department in one fell swoop with the tactical precision of Desert Storm, I was stripped of my corporate badges—credit card, calling card and employee I.D. card—and escorted out the side door. Lugging an overstuffed box of birthday cards and a potted plant my department gave me when I joined the firm, I stormed past a few stunned co-workers.*
>
> *Left behind in the employee kitchen was my farewell present to my colleagues, an uneaten chocolate birthday cake my boss made. She never got a slice either. In fact, despite her status as a corporate officer and her reputation*

as an indefatigable worker, she received the same pink-colored party favor I did.

By 10:30 a.m., the execution was complete. The corporate communications department was dead and buried officially. Out sourced, into oblivion. We had heard distant gunfire in the weeks before, but, as they say, we never saw the one that hit us smack in the head.

The new CEO—the fourth in five years—decided it would be cost effective to whack our entire department, quick and clean. No warning, no hints. It's better that way, or so the experts contend. Sore feelings can't fester into corporate sabotage. Never mind that for the first time in my otherwise unblemished 10-year career, I was facing a hostile job market minus the best leverage any worker has, a job.

To its credit, the company provided outplacement services and a small severance package worth about one month's salary. Later I pleaded for, and got, my tiny pension vested. Net value of my golden-years account: $1,500. Still, the scraps the company tossed my way couldn't overshadow the humiliation and disgrace I experienced on Black Monday.

From that day, I marched through the corporate world wearing a scarlet letter, while I networked and interviewed among the employed. "Laid off" my black mark beamed to the world. Each time I explained my situation people sympathized, recalling names of fallen comrades. Even so, I couldn't shake the feeling I'd been scarred permanently."

Steve has never been known to be a downer. Though he was soft-spoken and well mannered, he always had a passion to change the status quo. This is what prompted him to take risks with his life early on. Steve has always endured the trials and tribulations of the first generation immigrant with ease and grace. He knew there had to be a better approach that would ensure that he is never laid off again. "From now on, I will quit for reasons of my own, rather than be laid off because I do not have a job," Steve repeatedly told himself as he started searching for a better way.

* * *

Steve Wong, it appeared, had undergone a radical transformation. The experience of being laid off over two years ago had influenced him profoundly. It was a hard road to recovery. His self-confidence and pride were shattered. Never in his dreams had he envisioned that he could be the candidate for lay off. Yet, it happened, and he had to cope with it. Two years ago, he had been convinced that his education, college degree, his credentials as a top performer, and his testimonials from previous superiors were all that he needed as the platform for his employment and career growth. He had never failed in his assignments. His supervisors were always helpful in describing exactly what Steve needed to get done, and he always got the job done. Yet, he was faced with the dreadful experience of two years ago.

After the lay off, there was no one to tell Steve what to do. Everyone he contacted was appreciative of his credentials and background. Yet, no one seemed to want his services. The employment agents he contacted suggested that Steve was too highly specialized to meet their needs. This made no sense to Steve. "What was the point in getting a Ph.D. if I am not specialized?" he wondered. However, there was no answer. Everyone else seemed busy doing their own "thing."

As time went by, Steve began to unravel the mystery. After several interviews, discussions with a number of peer groups, and reading numerous materials, a picture began to emerge. Getting information and interacting with a cross-section of resources was now much more natural to Steve than it was two years ago. Steve realized that his in-depth knowledge in his field of study had been mistakenly characterized as "specialized" by those who could not see the use of such knowledge to their immediate needs. His extensive study at school has been used to frame him as a technical specialist. "I have not helped the situation or clarified my capabilities either," reflected Steve. His extensive studies and research always had a common theme: to find the basic or scientific issues pertaining to the problem at hand. While he had specialized in a particular subject area, Steve realized that his core competence was the ability to frame any problem in terms of its scientific content. Where he had no direct or personal knowledge, Steve had developed the skills or experience to get the needed information from a range of literature and other sources. While he could relate to the core competencies of "knowledge" and "experience" at an individual level, it was a hard road for Steve to recognize "people skills" as a core competence as well. Through a carefully cultivated and forced habit, he began to realize that solving a problem often requires more than relying on himself as a singular resource. He began to recognize that there are distinctions between ability to interact, communicate with, and influence a group of functionally related individuals towards a problem-solving process versus merely working as part of a team.

This transformation for Steve, from a task-oriented "specialist" to a problem solver with clearly identified core competencies, was the beginning of the process towards the System Approach. Soon he began to recognize the organizational core competencies, and in the end the core competencies of his enterprise. It was clear to Steve that his core competencies, while consistent, had to change with time. In recent years, these changes seemed to be occurring somewhat frequently. "Perhaps this is part of globalization," reflected Steve. Yet, he decided to stay ahead of the wave, rather than be caught up in the storm of changes again.

Towards this purpose, Steve developed a set of three scorecards. The first was to assess the core competencies of his enterprise and their impact on the needs of his organization (Figure 7.5). He developed it through careful and extended observations and dialogue with his superiors, peers, subordinates, supplier industries, end use customers, etc. With this scorecard in hand, Steve developed a schedule to periodically assess the enterprise, its changing needs, and the impact of these needs on his organization. The scorecard also helped Steve to identify projects and problems that were relevant for

166 • The System Approach

CORE COMPETENCE OF THE ORGANIZATION	CORE COMPETENCE OF THE ENTERPRISE		
	TECHNOLOGY	INFORMATION AUTOMATION	GLOBAL LOGISTICS
SCIENCE	Org. Need / Enterprise Need		
ENGINEERING			
MANAGEMENT			

Figure 7.5 • Steve Wong's scorecard for assessment of the changing needs of the enterprise and its translation into the needs of his organization in the context of globaliztion.

CORE COMPETENCE OF THE INDIVIDUAL	CORE COMPETENCE OF THE ORGANIZATION		
	SCIENCE	ENGINEERING	MANAGEMENT
KNOWLEDGE	Need for Indiv. Competence / Org. Need		
EXPERIENCE			
PEOPLE SKILLS			

Figure 7.6 • Steve Wong's assessment of the organizational needs and their translation into individual core competencies needed.

SELF ASSESSMENT OF CORE COMPETENCE	CORE COMPETENCE NEEDS : INDIVIDUAL		
	KNOWLEDGE	EXPERIENCE	PEOPLE SKILLS
KNOWLEDGE	Need / Self Assessment		
EXPERIENCE			
PEOPLE SKILLS			

Figure 7.7 • Steve Wong's personal development scorecard.

his organization and the enterprise. Through this process, Steve was no longer perceived as a technical specialist. Instead he was viewed as a technology manager with a keen sense of the industry and its changing needs. For his part, Steve began to see growing opportunities to utilize information automation and global logistics, in addition to his natural strength—technology.

As the next step, Steve had developed a second scorecard (Figure 7.6) in terms of the core competencies required of the individuals in the organization. This was the tool Steve used frequently in the effective resolution of the problem. Such problem resolution frequently took on different headings—projects, special assignments, database support, international collaboration, customer interface, marketing assignments, etc. Steve handled this diversity of activities by appropriate deployment of his three core competencies: knowledge, experience, and people skills. His discussions on performance appraisal had gradually transformed into the evaluation of this scorecard, the assessment of his individual core competencies, and their match to the core competence needs of Steve's organization.

Steve's third scorecard (Figure 7.7) was in many respects his personal professional development plan. This was the scorecard that he used to rate himself versus the core competence profile required of employees such as Steve by his organization. Very quickly, Steve recognized the interconnection between this scorecard and the other two. Through this process, it was evident that personal development is not a mere successive execution of learning tasks. Instead, it is a synergistic evolution of his skills, which integrated the needs of his organization and that of his employer (or the enterprise). To satisfy such needs, he recognized that every project he participated in became a problem-solving process, which in turn enhanced his core competencies. While he had extensive knowledge on certain core competence needs of his enterprise (product technology), it was obvious to Steve that his knowledge in terms of other technology areas (process, manufacturing, and applications technologies) was limited. The constant growth in information technology and the global expansion of his company also posed challenges to Steve in terms of his knowledge in these areas as his core competence. As a problem solver, Steve began to recognize the distinctions between knowledge and information resources. In this respect, his clarity of understanding between technical output and the system output also helped Steve acquire relevant knowledge without becoming an overburdened technical specialist. Through these experiences Steve began to develop a healthy respect and comfort level for the life long learning process and its deployment for the best use of his organization (Figure 6.2).

Ram Aravindan—Supervisor

Ram Aravindan was extremely proud and happy as he headed out to the plant that morning. He had worked on a project for the past two years, day and night. His working hours were so long that his colleagues wondered if he had a family, and what they thought of this workaholic. None of this bothered Ram. He had been asked to improve the productivity in the manufacturing operation. Ram was extremely smart, and as talented as any engineer. His boss was convinced that if someone could make major strides, it would be Ram. As a result, he was determined to achieve an 80% reduction in cycle time in the operation.

Ram wasted little time in meetings, except when it was required for consultation on technical matters. His boss had decided to give him freedom and independence. As a result, Ram was not bothered with distractions such as project update meetings or status review by management. Independent and successful, Ram was prepared to make the presentation to his management on how he has devised a solution to achieve their goal—80% reduction in cycle time in the assigned manufacturing operation. It required an investment of one million dollars. But, the pay-back seemed very good. Ram was convinced that he had the problem licked. Therein lay his pride and joy.

The review meeting progressed through the morning. Ram described in great detail the engineering aspects of the problem and the solution. He even joked about his colleagues, who looked at him suspiciously throughout the project. One of them had even said, "This company has never invested in a such large capital purchase. Ram, you are the guinea pig." The meeting ended far later than originally scheduled. Ram was convinced that he would get the approval. "Look at the number of detailed questions asked. Surely, everyone understands by now what we can do in this operation," Ram reflected as he drove home that day. But in the meeting the Product Manager seemed very quiet. He never raised any questions or concerns. This was a source of unease in Ram's mind, while he was reflecting on his project presentation.

A week later, Ram was called into his supervisor's office. "Have they approved the project and the investments?" asked Ram. "No," came the reply. "The design department has eliminated the need for this component. For two years, while we have been working to reduce the manufacturing cost, design has been looking into reducing the number of components. Besides, this company would never go for such a large capital investment, anyway," stated the supervisor. Ram was devastated. "Ram, the problem is deeper than that," continued the boss. "Because of redesign, half the manufacturing operations are eliminated and what is left is being shipped offshore. They have promised to take care of all of us. If I were you, I would cast the net outside," he ended.

Engineering was Ram's lifeblood. In the recent years, he had refined it even further, with a focus on manufacturing engineering. If he cannot survive in a company that manufactures widgets, what can he do for a living? "Don't they all talk about productivity increases? Show me anyone who can increase productivity by more than 80%. If that is not needed, what does 'productivity' really mean?" Ram questioned. He was determined to find answers. An impartial observer could have guessed the sensitivity on Ram's part. It had not been long since he had gone through an intense personal experience. Ram described it as the worst debacle of his professional career. Of course, along with these events came personal hardships for Ram.

• • •

After a few years Ram was a changed person. He was determined to proceed further only after a clear understanding of the output expectations of the problem he was dealing with. While he remained flexible as needed, his eye was always set on the output and value/benefits. Ram had become a company expert in identifying and distinguishing between the technical output and the system output. It was this search for the definition of the output and its appropriate delineation that resulted in an intense conversation with a junior engineer. Perhaps Ram's personal involvement was more intense because of his passion to communicate and utilize the concepts of technical and system outputs and their distinctions as a strategic aspect in the definition of the problem on hand.

He could not believe the naiveté of the recently hired engineer with whom he was working. This junior engineer came with impeccable credentials. He was a graduate of a highly acclaimed college, had an excellent academic record, and a strong will to succeed. Like many others in his profession, this engineer was ready to jump into action and make something happen. Ram wished to know what this engineer was planning to accomplish. What started as a simple conversation between the two soon led to an animated discussion.

"First you need to decide what you want to accomplish, and why? This might appear simple or elementary. But if the answers are of interest only to you or someone extremely familiar with the details of your problem, frequently it is a technical output, " explained Ram.

"Well, I intend to finish a report on this design project by month's end. This report will be my 'technical output' I suppose," said the junior engineer.

"Yes, perhaps. The report is just a summary of our knowledge and the documentation of pertinent information, " replied Ram.

"Then what is my real output?" continued the engineer, with a deep anguish in his voice.

"What are the conclusions of the study? What are your recommendations on the concept and details of the design? Is it in a package ready for use by our advanced engineering department? These and similar results will be your output," replied Ram.

"But you don't need to be bothered with these details. Wouldn't you trust me to get these details to advanced engineering?" asked the junior engineer.

"You are absolutely right," replied Ram. "The above are your technical outputs. To the extent you get them done in a timely and cost effective manner and make sure your results are of benefit to the advanced engineering department, your output would have transformed into the system output," continued

Ram, barely able to contain his enthusiasm. He was convinced that the junior engineer was well on his way towards systems thinking.

"Perhaps you are interested in getting my job done as you have described. But is your boss interested in the details of my design, its integration with advanced engineering, or its cost effectiveness?" asked the junior engineer.

"Sure my boss is interested," replied Ram. "But she may not be as concerned about the details of your design as you or I would be. She would be pleased if your output incorporates aspects that efficiently integrate your design features with the design output of others. She would also be pleased if such integration of design increases the efficiency of the process steps before and after. In many respects these are my technical outputs."

"I see a cascading of outputs. As long as I can focus on my work such that my outputs are aligned with the value/benefit to the company, as viewed by your boss, I will be focused on the system output," replied the junior engineer.

"You are on the right track," replied Ram. "But you need to remember that you, my boss, and I are all part of the same input/process/output system. Thus, your focus need not be what I am looking for or what my boss needs in terms of output. Instead, it should be what all of us collectively produce to meet the needs and wants of our investors, customers, suppliers, the employees, and the company itself. These are the system outputs," clarified Ram Aravidan.

"At the same time, in order to get your job done, you need my skills as well as those of everyone in the organization. In effect, we become a collective pool of resources, a cluster of core competencies, as we transform the inputs to outputs. We manage this clustering of core competencies by allocation of resources. In accounting parlance, we call this the budget or planning process," explained Ram.

Set in motion in the system oriented thought process, the conversation was difficult to stop. The intelligence and the good academic training of the junior engineer began to

Personal Concerns and the System Approach • 173

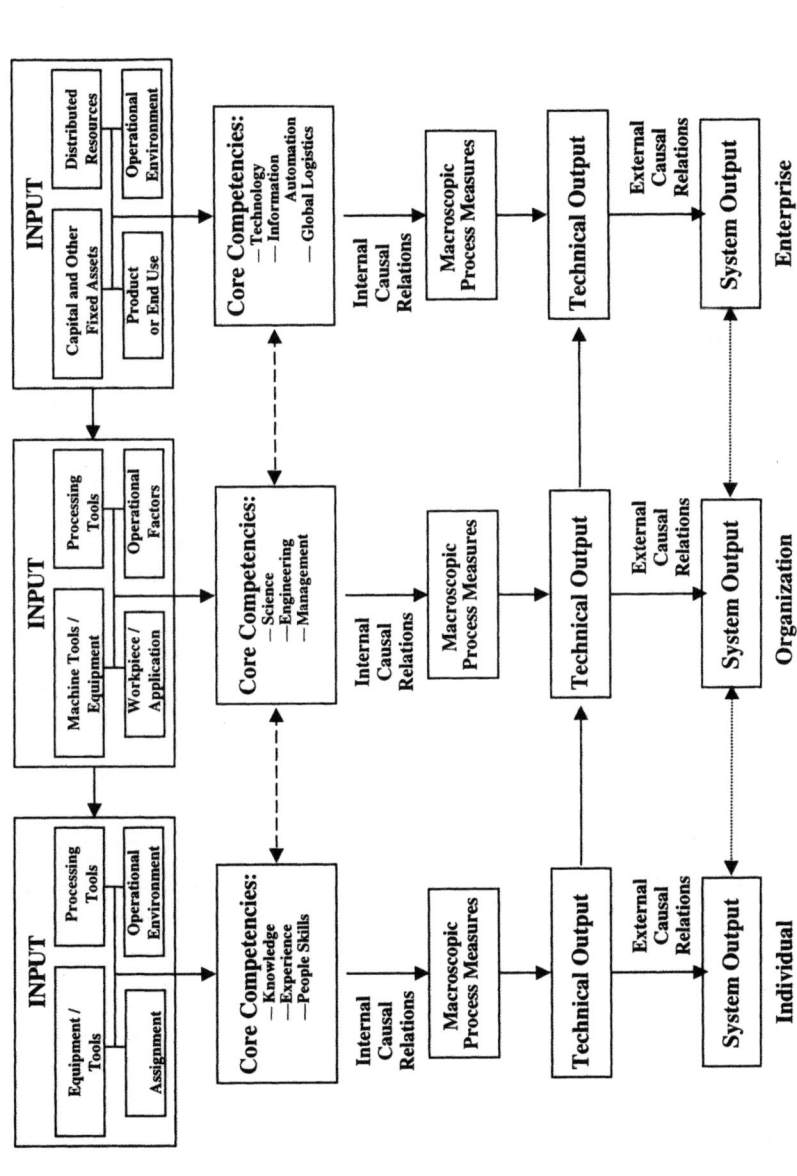

Figure 7.8 • Interrealtions between the system and its components between the various levels—individuals, organizations, and the enterprise.

come into effect in full force. What ensued was a collaborative learning process between Ram and the young engineer. When they were finished they could clearly see that they and other employees of the company were all part of the same input/process/output system with different and cascading scales of impact up and down the enterprise (Figure 7.8).

Henry Gonzalves—Product Manager

Henry Gonzalves was reflecting on his personal life. The business-class seat was comfortable aboard the transpacific commercial flight, and the service was excellent. Henry is a successful professional in a high technology company, based on the West Coast. His company has manufacturing operations in the Far East, which are duplicates of the West Coast operation. At least, in theory, they are supposed to be duplicates. But from day one, there were changes made to both operations.

One cannot say that those changes were not needed. Indeed, Henry has personally reviewed and approved each one. This flight is no different than the many he has taken before. Each was made in an attempt to address a process change or fix a process problem. His counterparts in both these locations normally take care of these changes, but that can work only if each location is committed to the larger overall goal. But that is not the case now. Hence, Henry has to travel every time a change is necessary. This is beginning to take a toll on his personal life, as he hardly has time to see his children. When he was promoted to Product Manager, Henry was warned that this could happen.

"I never realized how much of a toll business travel could take on my personal life, until now. And there's no end in sight. Unless," thought Henry, "there is a different way to implement process changes. Is there a way to give autonomy to local operations, while insisting that few overall objectives be met from the product point of view? Is there a common language at all locations that could make personal intervention by Product Managers like myself redundant?" he wondered.

The thought of a few less business trips and the chance of spending a Sunday with his son in the baseball field cheered Henry. He was committed to finding a common language that links research, product design, manufacturing, and customer use.

Henry Gonzalves reflected on his long career and many of his accomplishments. He was also mentally reviewing the process of successful product development. He is an expert in this field, having identified several market needs and then successfully developed products to meet these needs. He has good experience translating these products into commercial successes. This indeed was the reason Henry had been recently promoted. But, thanks to globalization, Henry seemed to be everywhere in the globe, constantly traveling all the time.

Through all his accomplishments in product development, Henry noticed a common theme. The impetus for a new product usually came from an identified market need. Usually there were many such needs. There were always more needs identified than money available. There was a well-established procedure to screen these opportunities, and gradually translate them into products through manufacturing, marketing, and sales. In every case of product development, it was ultimately the deployment of core competencies, delivered as value/benefit to the customers that made new products a success.

Henry's chance meeting with Mark Reardon and the conversations with him reinforced this point of view (Figure 7.1). The value/benefit of core competencies in terms of new product development was always the case of optimizing between a pair of functional requirements and their efficiency, as viewed by the customer in their use of the product. Translating the market needs in terms of the value/benefit needs of the customer seemed to be the critical first step in every product development effort. (Figure 7.9.) Once such a value/benefit map was identified, the new opportunity could then be refined. Sometimes it was incremental, opportunities for small-scale improvement. On occasion the opportunity was large, a "break through" opportunity.

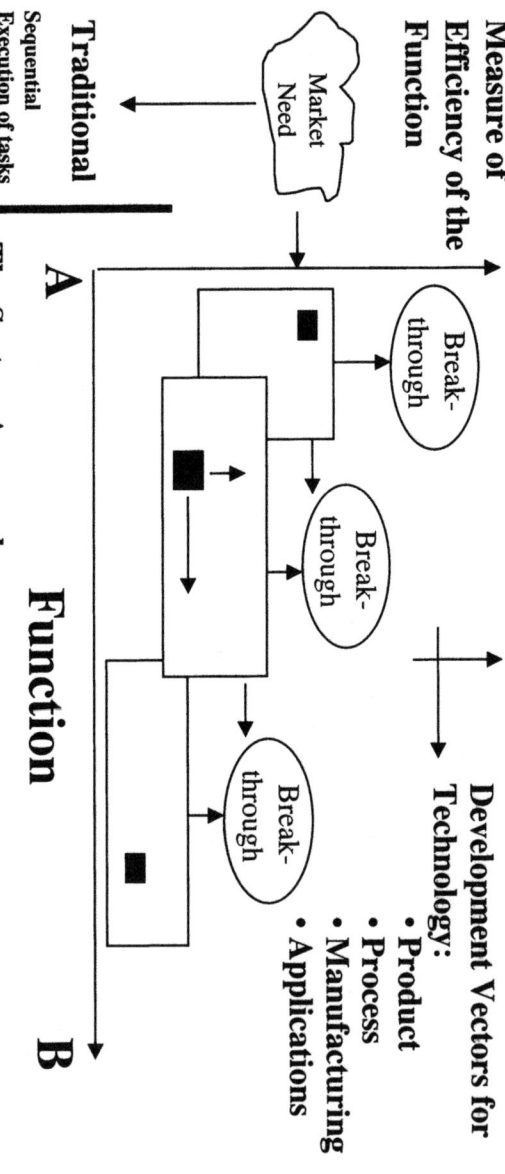

Figure 7.9 • System Approach for accelerated product development.

Mark Reardon had assured Henry that such a value/benefit map served as a common language to link all of his organizations, such as R&D, manufacturing, marketing and sales. (Figure 7.3.) Henry could see similar linkage in all of the operations in his company as well. In the past, each product development effort required attention to every detail pertaining to research, advanced engineering, manufacturing, marketing, and sales. Many times there were specialized resources in each of these functions. Henry was frequently called upon to deal with the constant conflict between the skill sets of the various teams versus the needs of the product development process. Much of his travel was frequently associated with this balancing of skills and team building among the resources.

The value/benefit map helped to identify the requirements in every business function upfront. They formed into natural teams (Figure 7.10). With the advent of competencies in information automation and global logistics, these teams began to give the impression of niche market operations in many respects, similar to Mark Reardon's system thinking (Figure 7.4). Ultimately, the product management process had evolved into a constant cycle of identifying the value/benefit needs of end customers' output, and meeting them through the core competencies at all levels.

Henry also recognized that a clear and comprehensive understanding of the technology of his company was essential. Such an understanding was critical to develop the value/benefit map. Such a map was critical in the understanding and deployment of all the core competencies of their global enterprise. Without such value/benefit mapping, the enterprise struggled through a series of task-oriented functions. Parallel processing and multiplexing of functions that were now natural to his enterprise looked amazing and difficult for their competitors.

Linda Sanchez—Production Worker

Linda Sanchez could not believe her ears. For the past fif-

178 • The System Approach

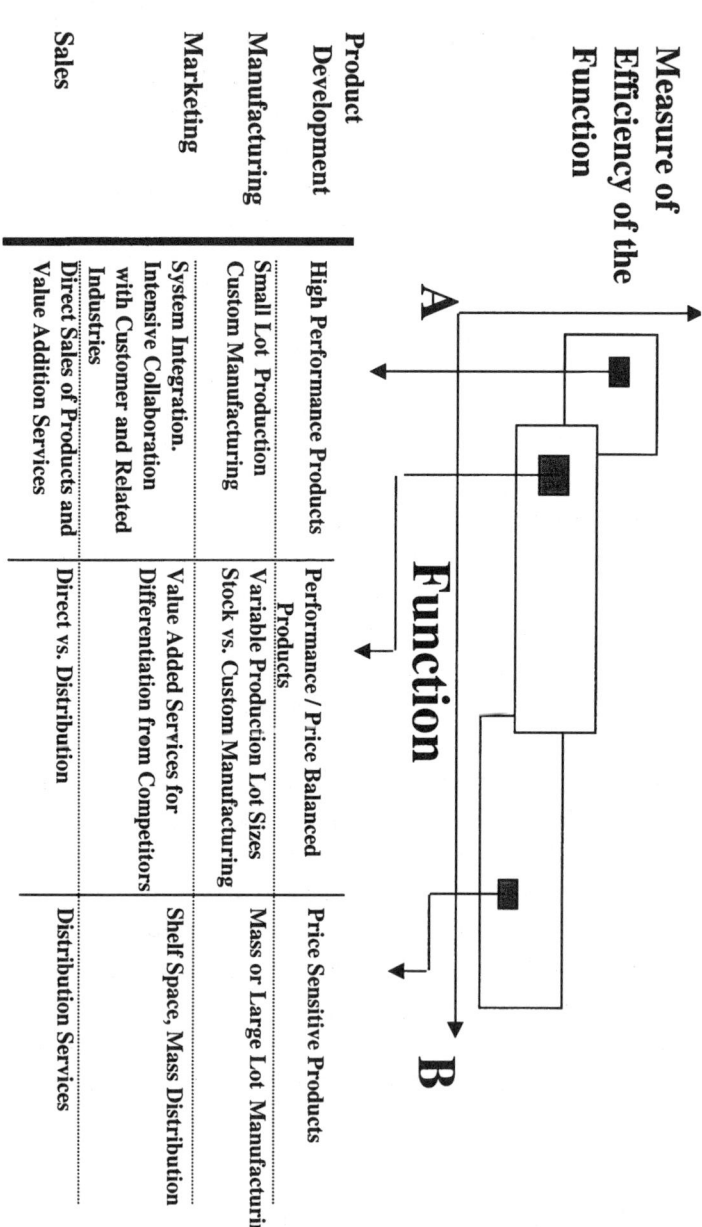

Figure 7.10 • Product Management through the System Approach results in development of informal and enterpreneurial and cross functional business teams as a natural response to meet the value/benefit needs.

teen years, she has not missed a single day at work. Her quality of work has always been impeccable. It was a week ago that the plant superintendent stopped by to shake hands and tell her that she was one of the best workers in this plant. Her job was precise. Mount the shaft in place, on the assembly line, and position it with the retaining spring. It was not up to her to ask why this assembly was needed. Nobody expected her to worry about it. Just get the job done, maintain the production rate, and never make a mistake was what she was told by the line foreman when she started this job. She had done exactly that for the past fifteen years, without missing a beat.

This morning, as she walked into the plant there was commotion all around. Everyone was doing their job, but no one seemed to have their mind on their work. Everyone had heard the same rumor. The company had decided to continue the design and development—the upstairs jobs that Linda knew only as the front office—but subcontract all production to a smaller company whose production lines have been making shafts and springs. It was only a matter of adding a few operations to finish the sub-assembly.

"What am I supposed to do now?" Linda wondered. She could not just pick up her family and move, even if she wanted to. What about the new company? "Do they have a job for me? And if they do, how long will it last?" thought Linda. There was no end to Linda's questions and concerns.

Linda Sanchez always knew that she had a keen sense of understanding and analysis of problems, both on and off the job. With the limited earnings she had, Linda had wisely invested her small savings, which helped to pay for the down payment for her home. She could also help her children in their homework, as she enjoyed learning. Linda had always been active in the Parent Teacher Association of the local school and many other projects in her small town. She participated in and enjoyed all of them. She didn't have to think twice about her job, as the company she was working for had always been there.

• • •

That was four years ago. The plant she had worked for had moved south. She had to find a new job. The road to recovery had not been easy. Now, Linda Sanchez was no longer a production worker. Long gone were the days when Linda was called an assembly line worker. Instead, her new job title has become Asset Manager—Production Operations.

It was through sheer luck that Linda ran into Mark Reardon in the local grocery store. Linda had known about Mark and his new approach in running his enterprise. She had wanted to meet him to express her sense of anguish and anger. But, by the time Linda finally meet Mark, much of her personal concern had been transformed. Through serious reflection, she had been able to understand the details of globalization. She was more upset with herself for not having seen the big picture earlier. Now she was looking for an opportunity.

"The chance meeting with Mark was the best thing that happened in my life," Linda could be heard saying out loud and often. "The rest of it is history." After they met, Mark had offered her a production line job. Through careful reflection, Linda recognized that the experience of working on the shop floor, and the people skills she had gained by working with a cross-section of people, were her core competencies. She realized that her knowledge of industrial processes and practice was limited. She had decided to build on her core competence.

While she was hired as a helper in the machining department, Linda began to gain knowledge of machining processes through reading books and talking to engineers and other coworkers. Of course, Mark had created a climate that encouraged such knowledge building processes. She took the opportunity for training, whenever the opportunity came along. With her hands-on skills and keen focus to gain knowledge, it was not long before Linda assumed the job of machinist. She started learning the use of computers. She had little or no knowledge of the inner-workings of the computer. Yet she became a wizard in operating computers and using them for various functions, many of them connected with CNC machine tools. As far as Linda was concerned, she was a skilled machinist. In her view, CNC machines had a high level of information automation. CNC machines helped her to achieve results.

Linda would describe her job like this: "I am a surface generation technologist using machining tools equipped with information automation devices."

Linda also had a keen interest in the operation of the company in various parts of the world. She was increasingly aware of customers, competitors, and suppliers of the company on a worldwide basis. If anyone wanted to know something about the company, Linda had a way of finding out through her contacts, the Internet, or whatever. They were all her resources of global logistics.

One day when Mark Reardon walked by the floor, Linda said, "Why not combine those two machines now located in far off corners in one location. If you could add one more machine, I could program, operate, and manage all three machines myself. This will also improve cost efficiency as well as flexibility to meet custom orders, when required."

Before Mark could pause for a second, Linda pulled out a cost justification package she had worked out with the financial controller. Mark was truly amazed. As a shrewd businessperson, he could not overlook the opportunity. The project was approved. Linda helped oversee all aspects of the project.

In the most sincere way possible, Mark asked Linda, "What should we call this job you do?"

Linda Sanchez had no hesitation. "Why not call me Asset Manager—Production Operations?" Isn't that what I do?" asked Linda. Mark had no problem with the answer.

As the enterprise manager committed to the System Approach, Mark Reardon worked with the Human Resource Manager until the appropriate changes were made in the title, as well as the compensation for Linda. After all, Linda was not merely a production worker. She was part of the enterprise management team. Linda had also changed her outlook on life. She was much more involved with her children, their education, and their long-term career development. She worked hard with the local school system to see the big picture and modify their educational programs more towards developing core competencies rather than just mere learning of a set of academic topics. Similar to Steve Wong (Figures 7.5, 7.6, and 7.7), in her own way Linda had developed scorecards for assessment of her enterprise, organization, and herself.

Paul Bloomberg—Professor

Professor Paul Bloomberg had just finished reading an article, and laid the journal on top of a pile of other reading materials. Surrounding him were stacks of papers, publications, and journal articles. Indeed, he had personally contributed to several of them. He was proud of the fact that he had published over 200 articles in various journals jointly with a host of others. A healthy number of these co-authors came from his steady stream of students; and many of them had gone on to further teaching or to work as engineers employed in large industries.

Dr. Bloomberg reflected on the article that he had just finished reading.[17] The words were clear and precise in his memory.

> *On paper at least, the engineering profession is thriving. According to the most recent bi-annual report on the engineering job market by the U.S. Bureau of Labor Statistics (BLS), issued in November 1995, the unemployment rate for engineers is, at less than 2 percent, the lowest it's been since the last recession, in 1991. On top of that, more engineers are employed than ever before.*
>
> *"It's puzzling, too," says Dick Ellis, a sociologist who has analyzed the BLS engineering employment data for the American Association of Engineering Societies in Washington, D.C. "More engineers are employed than ever before,*

but we also know that work is continuing to move offshore, and some of the work performed here is being done by engineers with temporary visas. Thus, demand appears to be sufficient to replace what's moving offshore, absorb additional entrants to the labor market, and still keep engineering unemployment historically low."

Despite the plethora of positive signs, for too many mechanical engineers today's boom still resembles all too closely the bust of the early 1990s. Plummeting demand for defense products and ongoing reengineering are just two factors prolonging the wave of corporate downsizing that started during the last recession. Furthermore, even some of the increases in employment reflect contract or temporary work, which in many cases does not provide health and other benefits.

Ellis also pointed to the relatively narrow gap between current employment levels and those projected for 2005. According to the BLS's most recent bi-annual report, there will be 2,315,853 engineers and engineering managers in the United States in 2005, an increase of 503,358 over 1994's 1,812,495. "Considering that we're already just about at the 2 million mark, we don't have too far to grow," he said.

"It's not a very optimistic forecast," Ellis added. "The BLS has been getting more conservative in its estimates for engineering employment."

"Not only is downsizing continuing," Ellis said, but "on top of that, about 1 million engineering graduates are joining the labor force around the world each year. That means that every two years, about as many engineers are added to the world labor market as are employed in total in the United States."

Computer and telecommunications technologies are making it easier for U.S.-based companies to tap this growing labor force. " Companies are using powerful computers to link engineers at sites all over the world," he added. "As a result, engineers don't have to be in the same geographic *location to collaborate on a project."*

All told, the falling demand for defense products, continued downsizing, increasing globalization, and a rapidly expanding engineering labor market worldwide mean that "as much as times have improved, this still is not a time for engineers to relax," Ellis said.

The movement of engineering employment from large companies to small and midsize ones is perhaps the most noticeable trend of all, according to the directors of ASME's regional offices.

The rise of small and midsize business has also been accompanied by a change in employer expectations of mechanical engineers. "Small and midsize companies want a systems individual," he said. "They don't have teams of engineers, and they don't have specialists. They need one person who has the flexibility to do it all—all the way from idea to implementation."

"Service firms are looking for generalists with flexibility," Ellis said. "That means an ability to work for any client. If you can combine the knowledge of engineering and business, you become much more interesting to an employer."

In the past, employers placed a high value on hiring graduates with good grades," said Ellis. "Now, companies want graduates who can work as a team, have good communications skills, and have project experience.

"That's particularly true for small companies, where there are fewer people and the ability to work with others is so important," he added. "Engineering skills are still critical—especially if you're going into consulting and need to be on an equal footing with specialists employed by your clients. Even then, MEs are expected to be able to quickly grasp their clients' business problems, so generalists still have an edge."

The daunting prospect of graduating more engineers in a shrinking marketplace concerned Professor Bloomberg. All his contacts were at large companies. His research initiatives and funding support came from large companies. His research endeavors were focused on meeting the needs of large companies. In order to be successful in the future, it would appear that he needed to focus on small- and medium-sized companies, if he were to believe what he had just finished reading. The sentence, *"small- and medium-sized companies want a system individual,"* reverberated in his thoughts.

"What is a system individual? How does he/she differ from the engineers I have graduated?" he asked himself. He was also intrigued by the statement, *"if you can combine the knowledge of engineering and business, you become more interesting to the employer."*

Even after 30 years of a distinguished career at his university, Professor Bloomberg had never once stepped inside the School of Management. "Well, none of my colleagues from that school—'that far away land' was how the school of management was referred to in his close circles—have ever stopped by to chat with us at the School of Engineering, have they?" reasoned Professor Bloomberg.

He knew of several of his students who had gone on to business degrees after engineering education. But he could not recall any situation where business majors had ever come to the engineering school for higher education or even taken continuing education courses. He even recalled conversations where his colleagues had lectured to engineering students to focus on specific problem-solving.

"Engineering is a quantitative process. Engineers should not be swayed by the 'touchy, feely' aspects of management and its uncertainties," thought Professor Bloomberg, who had heard it said so often. "Maybe there is a different approach to combine engineering and management education, from early on. Perhaps, then, students can save the expense and time of obtaining independent degrees in engineering and management. More importantly, the best of both disciplines is integrated, so that students in this competitive market develop the versatility to handle a range of opportunities better than their counterparts from other parts of the world. Is there a role for combining science, engineering, and management in an integrated education to develop the systems individuals of the future?" Although not known for his readiness to change, Professor Bloomberg was known to be unstoppable once he set his course and direction.

• • •

One year later, Professor Paul Bloomberg had just finished a detailed study. He had undertaken the project after his serious reflection on the state of higher education and where it should be headed to meet the changing needs of the global marketplace. The study had been thorough and extensive. It involved meetings and discussions with his former students, colleagues, employers, research organizations, professional societies, and many other sources. He made sure that his resources were as broad as possible. As a result of this study, he came to the conclusion that his profession as a teacher included the responsibility of increasing the core competence of his students in terms of knowledge. He could see this as the common theme for any and every person involved in the teaching process, and that it should be implemented from early childhood education all the way up to the highest levels of graduate school and beyond into the continuing education process.

Based on his recent studies, Professor Bloomberg concluded that the output of all industrial processes would appear to be the result of an appropriate and logical deployment of core competencies at every level—from the individual to the enterprise. This connection between the sources of knowledge and their linkage to the core competencies was apparent (Figure 3.5).

Professor Bloomberg reminded himself that there is not a simple linear connection or ascendancy of core competencies from individuals through the organization to the enterprise. In traditional industries, there has been an arbitrary linkage among the nine core competencies. But in a global, system-oriented enterprise, each core competence at any level is a mutual integration of all three core competencies from the level below. The integration of knowledge seemed to mirror the integration of core competencies, as discussed earlier (Figure 5.10).

Professor Bloomberg further reflected on the education or process of knowledge building. He asked, "If all industrial activities are an 'input/process/output' system, then what are the distinctions in the level of knowledge required to participate in the process? Is it merely the case of being related to the size of the system? Does it mean an individual with responsibility for a large system has greater accumulation of knowledge than someone below? How does such gathering of knowledge differ from the traditional views of generalists and specialists?" he pondered.

Professor Bloomberg concluded that traditional industrial employment is classified between blue-collar and white-collar workers. This is largely based on the degree of deployment of physical skills versus knowledge-based know-how. Within each category, individuals perform certain specified tasks. Where specification of the tasks is not clearly spelled out, arbitrary choices of the tasks are used, with segmentation based on organizations and their functions. Individuals or organizations that acquire or demonstrate higher levels of capabilities within a task are called specialists. On the other hand, individuals or organizations with demonstrated skills or capabilities over a wider range of tasks are called generalists. Specialists are presumed to have in-depth knowledge of a subject, while generalists are presumed to have shallow knowledge on a diversity of subjects. In reality, knowledge is confined to specific tasks in the case of both specialists and the generalists.

Based on his recent studies, it became apparent to Professor Bloomberg that such distinctions are becoming blurred and, to some extent, extinct. This transition has been the consequence of the use of information automation and global logistics as core competencies by industries, as noted in Chapter 2. It is also clear that within jobs at every level there is an input/process/output system with a focus on quantum improvements in the system output.

It became apparent to Professor Bloomberg that the recognition of the input/process/output system in all our activities will be the first requirement in the global economy. This awareness of the system will involve its description in terms of its input components, core competencies, measures of core competencies, and their manifestations in terms of the technical and system output (Figure 6.6). To the extent this awareness of the system is comprehensive, the questions raised related to the system will also be more relevant and comprehensive. Such awareness also creates a natural process of seeking relevant resources needed to solve the problem pertinent to the system with a keen eye on improving the system output. The mere capability or awareness of the system view of the process transforms an individual, organization, or enterprise from a task execution function to a problem resolution function.

The mere awareness of the system perspective of the process facilitates natural alliances between related resources pertinent to the system (Figures 4.8 and 5.7). Interdisciplinary teams are formed as a consequence of such system thinking. Professor Bloomberg observed that interdisciplinary thought process is the critical need to solve the problem on hand. Interdisciplinary teams, when they are formed in any organization, must become agents to facilitate such interdisciplinary thought processeses.

Professor Bloomberg was thinking of concepts of teamwork and concurrent engineering. How do they differ from the System Approach? He concluded that in our task-oriented society and organization, transfer of information and logistics take enormous time and resources. In such a process, it becomes necessary to establish the standards for collection, processing, and dissemination of information. Similar rigors are required in all transfer activities or logistics. Previously, such efforts were streamlined through cross-functional teams. These teams served as facilitators to reduce redundancies in activities between well-defined departments and organizations. As tools of information automation and global logistics evolved, computer-based tools have helped create such cross-functional organizations. These activities have come to be identified as concurrent engineering. Yet, organizations have continued to be an assemblage of tasks.

In the System Approach the focus is on the individual and his/her commitment to interdisciplinary thought process, with a goal of quantum changes in the system output. The team formation occurs not for the purpose of assemblage of task-oriented specialists. Instead, teamwork becomes a natural outcome with a common commitment to the expanded use of core competencies at every level—individual, organization, and enterprise—to achieve quantum changes in the system outputs.

"Beyond the mere awareness of the process as a system, how does one address the end objective of solving the problem?" asked Professor Bloomberg. He recognized that solving the problem is a mere expression of modulating the system output. Internal causal relations, as well as the external causal relations pertinent to the system influence this. External causal relations in a traditional economy are measured largely in terms of marketplace and its response to the technical outputs of the enterprise. However, in a global economy the external causal relations assume many aspects. Professor Bloomberg decided to explore these external causal relations of the enterprise as part of his future studies.

Professor Bloomberg then reflected on the internal causal relations of the system. Trained as a scientist and researcher, he could relate to these readily. Indeed, his accomplishments as a scientist have been focused on uncovering these causal relations in his chosen field of study. Many of his studies in the past have been mere articulations of the system and its components. Only a few of his studies have extended the scientific principles or governing relationships. Professor Bloomberg recognized these few studies immediately, as they seemed to have had the greatest impact and were perceived as his best accomplishments. Invariably, he had been able to solve many industrial problems by repeated applications of these principles. He also recognized that the knowledge of these internal causal relations and the ability to deploy them to solve the problem on hand was at a level higher than the mere awareness or ability for description of the problem as a system.

Professor Bloomberg concluded that the knowledge of the internal and external causal relationships of the system and their use for solving the problem to achieve quantum changes in the system output is at a level higher than the mere awareness of the problem as a system. He decided to call this the "analysis capability." (Figure 6.6.) The knowledge pertaining to analysis of the system become readily apparent when the system output is modulated with a high degree of predictability. This is accomplished by effective deployment of core competencies within the system—individual, organization, and/or the enterprise—along with a logical influence on the internal and external causal relationships. The analysis capability is best recognized when the system can be duplicated, tested, or experimented with at a high degree of reliability.

"What could be higher than the knowledge of analysis of the industrial process as a system?" wondered Professor Bloomberg.

Through the process of analysis, one can alter or modulate the output of existing systems. Is it possible to configure and integrate new solutions or novel systems based on clearly identified system outputs and with due consideration for the internal and external causal relations? This would require a total comprehension of the input groups and their assemblage to obey the defined internal and external causal relations. This, in many respects, will involve creating new systems or new solutions, which heretofore have not been conceived. Their creation is not merely conceiving of possible new concepts, but a systematic representation of the concept on smaller scale, verification, and, finally, transforming the concept into full-scale and functioning systems with the desired system outputs. This level of knowledge Professor Bloomberg decided to call the "synthesis capability." (Figures 6.6.)

In due course, Professor Bloomberg concluded that knowledge in any form of education consisted of three levels—awareness, analysis, and synthesis of the input/process/output system. The systems themselves could exist in hundreds and thousands of configurations. Many traditional disciplines and fields of study contributed to these systems, depending on the nature and type of industry under which the system in consideration existed. But the knowledge pertaining to any and all of these disciplines and their interconnected fields always could be grouped under these three categories—awareness, analysis, and synthesis of industrial processes or input/process/output systems.

Chapter 8
A Glimmer of Hope

It was an extraordinary meeting on a spring morning. Paul Gagnon had been asked to chair this meeting. At first it was not clear to Paul why he had been chosen, but events were beginning to clearly unfold along a logical pattern.

After his bad dream (Chapter 1), Paul had been in relentless search for a better tomorrow. As a result, he was looking for anyone and everyone who could help him to explain the concerns he had visualized in his bad dream. As luck would have it, he had been brought into contact with Linda Sanchez, a factory worker like Paul, now functioning as Asset Manager—Production Operations (see Chapter 7). Linda, in turn, had introduced Paul to her company president, Mark Reardon. Mark had not only turned his company around as a dynamic leader, but he was happy to share his views on this transformation. Paul, in his relentless pursuit of finding a better way, had taken the extraordinary step of introducing

Mark Reardon to Jack Singer, the President of the company. Needless to say Linda Sanchez, with her sincere commitment to the System Approach, was enormously helpful to Paul in accomplishing these introductions.

At first Jack was highly skeptical. He had enough problems of his own. He did not need another approach or methodology. However, he was desperate—willing to try almost anything to survive and succeed in the global economy. Also, the sincere commitment and perseverance of Paul and Linda had really moved Jack. He held fond memories of the "good old days," when he himself was a production worker.

What happened next saved the company. The System Approach became the new paradigm in Jack Singer's company. Everyone was talking about it. There were even pockets of stability in various parts of his organization, often credited to the System Approach. Jack wanted everyone to keep him informed about what was going on. Hence, he had called this meeting and he felt it was appropriate to have Paul Gagnon chair this meeting, since he had been instrumental in getting this transformation started. Jack also felt that through this assignment he could truly show his commitment to the process of problem-solving. His allegiance to organization, structure, and hierarchy were a thing of the past. He was now a man driven with a new mission. He wanted to solve the problem and not merely execute the task.

"Thank you Mr. Singer," Paul said, as he opened the meeting. "I am truly honored to have been asked to chair this meeting. We all know that meetings are nothing more than means to collect, process, and disseminate information. In keeping with our need to deploy information as strategically as possible, Jack has asked everyone to share their recent experiences regarding our transition to the System Approach. Perhaps it is best to go around the room. Thanks to the tools of information automation and global logistics, we have several participants in this meeting from various locations of the world. Yet, for our purpose, our room will be a single, 'virtual room.' Your turn will be determined by where your images appear, either through physical presence, through the video monitor, or simply from the audio input."

Paul's last few sentences were very complicated. Yet, for everyone in the virtual room, it was extremely clear as each one was focused on the overall objective, which was sharing the knowledge and experience on the use of the System Approach as a problem-solving tool to survive and succeed in the global economy.

"Perhaps we can begin with Mr. Singer," concluded Paul.

"As a result of globalization, or as a consequence of the global economy, there seem to be two observations which are clear in my mind," began Jack Singer with his extraordinary summary of the System Approach.

1. "In order to support the highest standard of living, the value or benefit of any effort has to be the highest achievable anywhere in the world.
2. Conversely, the rewards for any effort will support a person living a country with the lowest standard of living anywhere in the world where the effort can be accomplished.

"Both these observations are extensions of the laws of economics we all have studied. What is new is the expansiveness of the resource to be used—from anywhere in the world, instead of from pockets or selected locations.

"Taken in a negative perspective, the above seems to predict a hopeless degeneration into the future. On the other hand, there are three tools available to benefit from globalization. This leads to our next observation.

3. Technology, information automation, and global logistics are the three core competencies of any enterprise in the global economy.

"In the past, arbitrary deployment of any of these three core competencies was adequate. In a global economy, it is necessary to deploy all three core competencies simultaneously. (Figure 3.5.) Any enterprise that deploys these three core competencies, simultaneously and better than anyone else in the world, will be the world leader.

"I have often wondered why this process of globalization has come into place now, and not a few decades earlier. In many respects, it is a natural outgrowth of developments in information, communications, and transportation technologies. The impact of these technologies on our enterprises can be grouped under two areas—information automation and global logistics.

"We have always had information to deal with. Today we can collect, process, disseminate, and deploy information faster and better than ever before. This ability is information automation as a core competence. (Figure 2.4.)

"We have always had logistics to contend with. This capability now expands far beyond movement of raw materials and physical goods. This ability to move and deploy resources of any kind on a worldwide basis has emerged into a new core competence—global logistics. (Figure 2.4.)

"At this point I would like to state these observations:

4. As global enterprises saturate the deployment of the core competencies of information automation and global logistics, there will be an extraordinary spurt in the growth of technology. But for those external to the enterprise such rapid changes in one among the three core competencies will not be obvious, as the effective global enterprise will deploy all three core competencies in a synergistic manner.

5. Technology can be divided between four categories, (a) product, (b) process, (c) manufacturing, and (d) applications. The applications technology, the least exploited among the four, will become a strategic tool for any enterprise, particularly when it is well integrated with other technologies and other core competencies. Such integration is an imperative for any successful global enterprise.

6. The successful global enterprise may not be a single entity with dedicated resources in fixed locations. Instead, the global enterprise in order to be successful will exploit the core competencies—technology, information auto-

mation, and global logistics—in any necessary combinations around the world with appropriate resources within the enterprise, as well as its suppliers and end-users, modulated from its various locations around the world. (Figure 6.4.)

7. The ability to modulate worldwide resources is highly unstable if we are focused on technical outputs, which are merely the means to the end. The end, of course, is the system outputs, or the stakeholder benefits: (a) investor's ROI, (b) employee benefits and growth, (c) success of the end-user industries, (d) success of the supplier industries, and (e) long-term viability of the enterprise itself. These are the value or benefits of the enterprise. To the extent there is focus on the system output, the process of managing the enterprise acquires greater stability. Such stability is of long-term nature, if the enterprise seeks quantum changes or large scale improvements in all of the above five system outputs and not merely on arbitrarily chosen few.

"As a final remark:

8. Achieving quantum improvements (a different mousetrap) in all the system outputs is nearly impossible in a task-oriented, traditional enterprise. It is possible only through a system-oriented enterprise where everyone is involved. All employees of the enterprise, the supplier industries and the end-user industries, are focused on the same objectives, i.e., to achieve quantum improvements in all the system outputs, through simultaneous deployment of the three core competencies—technology, information automation, and global logistics—at every level.

"At this point, I request that Mr. Joe Whitehead, our Product/Process Technology Manager, present his observations," Mr. Singer concluded.

"I'm Joe Whitehead. My department is responsible for helping the enterprise-wide exploitation of product and process technologies. My new title is Product/Process Technology

Manager. This is a transition from my previous task-oriented assignment as the Manager, Design Department. I would like to continue on the observations on the System Approach, outlined earlier by Mr. Singer.

9. Every enterprise has inputs, which can be broadly grouped under four categories: (a) fixed assets or those directly linked to large scale or discrete investments of money or capital; (b) variable or distributed resources, which can be relatively easily moved or reassigned to and from any location in the world; (c) application, or end use which is to be satisfied, and (d) operational factors or environment. (Figure 4.4.)

"Clearly, these four inputs are not all physical objects or easily classified in financial terms alone. Yet, clarification of all the inputs in these four categories is a must to understand the enterprise as an input/process/output system.

10. All organizations in an enterprise are a subset of the same system, described by the enterprise. (Figure 5.6.) Thus every organization within an enterprise has its share of inputs, which can be classified under the above four input groupings.
11. The objective of an enterprise is to integrate the four input groupings through the enterprise level core competencies—technology, information automation, and global logistics—to achieve quantum improvements in the system output. The organizations utilize the subsets of the same four input groupings. They integrate these inputs through each of the above three core competencies of the enterprise simultaneously. To accomplish this, the organization level core competencies are used. These are: science, engineering, and management. The objective of such deployment of core competencies at the organization level is the same as at the enterprise level, i.e., achieve or maximize the improvements in the system outputs.
12. While the enterprise has three core competencies to deal with, the organization has its three core compe-

tencies, which support all of the three core competencies of the enterprise in a matrixed fashion. In the traditional economy, excellence in any arbitrary combination of the two sets of core competencies was adequate. In a global economy, what is needed is a simultaneous deployment of all three of the core competencies of the organization in synergy with all the three core competencies of the enterprise.
13. Any organization that integrates all three of its core competencies with each of the enterprise level core competencies achieves success in the globalized economy. This simultaneous deployment leads to clusters of core competencies without clearly defined organizational boundaries or barriers.

"To date, development of such clusters of core competencies is largely focused on information automation and global logistics. In our task-oriented approach, we identify them through different terms such as continuous improvement, cross-functional teams, concurrent engineering, and business process reengineering, etc.
14. As an organization-level manager, my goal is to deploy the core competencies of science, engineering, and management, as they pertain to the technology, information automation, and global logistics of our enterprise, with an objective of achieving quantum improvements in the system outputs of our enterprise. In order to accomplish this, we need individuals, everyone in the enterprise at every level, to have a set of core competencies.

"At this time, I would like Ms. Mary Patterson to describe the core competencies of individuals in the System Approach," concluded Joe Whitehead.

"I am Mary Patterson. My title is Manufacturing Process Professional. I am not a scientist, engineer, or manager. I am focused on all of the aspects of my organization, as required. I get involved in manufacturing process problems with one goal, to identify the strategic importance of the problem in terms of the system outputs and achieve larger system outputs once the problem is resolved.

"In the beginning, it was difficult to follow these ideas. I was much happier to run from problem to problem. One day Joe asked me, 'How many problems are you involved in today?' I told him, over fifteen! I was glad he asked, as I was wearing thin with all this running around.

"Joe suggested, 'Of these fifteen, which of them will have the most impact for our company as well as to our customers?' I had never thought of it that way. I suppose that is what strategic thinking is all about. Since that day, I decided that I would think for myself rather than letting my supervisor do the thinking on my behalf. Joe told me, Mary, you are transforming into a manager, already." Everyone in the virtual room burst into laughter. They all agreed that management is a method of looking at the problem, and that is everybody's job.

"I have also been challenged by Paul Gagnon" Mary continued. "There was a problem on the production floor. I kept going at it with one failed solution after another. One day Paul told me, 'Mary we have to get to the bottom of the problem. Do we really understand why this problem occurs? I don't mean understanding it enough to fix it for one day or a few days.' In other words, Paul was looking for a robust solution based on the 'science' of the problem. It took us a while. We had to get a lot of help and learn a lot for ourselves. But now when I fix a problem, I don't have to go back to it for at least a couple of years. There is really no magic to it. Many of the problems are driven by a few basic scientific principles. When you understand the science behind the problem, you can duplicate it in the laboratory. Test the problem and the solutions from all perspectives. Sometimes you don't have to test everything. This is where your intuition, like the engineer's, comes into play. I can translate the solutions into shop floor use faster, because my resources are unlimited and worldwide. The suppliers and end-users are constantly willing to help me, as they benefit more from my integrated approach to solve the problem by the simultaneous use of science, engineering, and management.

"I am not unique in this. Everyone in our organization thinks this way. We are not a team of individuals. Instead, we are a pool of collective thinkers and problem solvers, relying on science, engineering, and management principles as and when required. Joe frequently calls us a 'cluster of core competencies.'

"The way we got to this process of the System Approach was rather simple. After my discussions with Joe, I asked myself, 'Why am I running around like this all the time?' It was clear that I was afraid of losing my job. Hence, I wanted to get as many things done as possible. This is what I have been trained for all along. Get the job done. But the job has always been tasks or bits and pieces of a problem. Defining the problem in its entirely, before embarking on it, was missing. In fact, nobody even encouraged it or took the time to explain how to define the problem. We were all task-oriented individuals, rather than system-oriented problem solvers. (Figures 2.6 and 2.7.) Once we recognized this need, the change process was easy.

"Perhaps now, I should list my observations on the System Approach in line with those of Jack Singer and Joe Whitehead.

15. The core competencies of any organization—science, engineering, and management—are in many respects a reflection of the competencies of individuals in that organization.
16. Every industrial activity can be described as a subset of the input/process/output system. The core competencies of the enterprise, organizations, and the individuals, are utilized to integrate the input/process/output system.
17. The outputs of the system, if they are perceived from the limited view of the organization, are identified as the 'technical outputs.' On the other hand, if the outputs can be related to a larger perspective of the orga-

nization and its role within the enterprise, the 'system outputs' are then identified.

18. The inputs for any process can be grouped under four categories, namely: machine tools or fixed assets, processing tools or distributed resources, application, and operational factors or operational environment. Simultaneous integration of all these four input groupings, with due respect for pertinent scientific principles, always lead to quantum changes in the system output.

19. In the System Approach, individuals acquire and deploy three core competencies—knowledge, experience, and people skills. These individual core competencies have to be integrated, synergistically, to achieve the desired organizational core competencies of science, engineering, and management which, in turn, are deployed by the enterprise through its core competencies of technology, information automation, and global logistics. (Figure 3.5.)

20. Thus, we have three sets of core competencies at three levels—the individual, the organization, and the enterprise. In the past, excellence in any arbitrary combination was adequate. In the global economy, it is necessary to integrate all the three core competencies at every level and in synergy with the level above, as this leads to the highest value or benefit. (Figures 6.1 and 6.2.)

21. Experience is not the skill acquired by the repetitive execution of the same task. Experience in the System Approach is the core competence of an individual acquired through personal involvement in defining the problem. Analyzing the problem and the resultant deployment of core competencies, leading to quantum changes in the system outputs and/or synthesis of new solutions, is the answer.

22. People skills, as a core competence of individuals, go beyond the ability to interact and interface with people,

particularly those who are familiar or those with whom we come into personal contact. In a global economy where resources are deployed from anywhere in the world, people skills really mean thinking on behalf of and relating to people anywhere in the world, with their cultural and economic diversity and preferences. This ability to connect with or develop relationships with people around the world is required more frequently through various and virtual media, as an enterprise deploys its core competencies of information automation and global logistics, as part of globalization.

23. Knowledge as an individual competence also acquires new meaning in a global economy. It is not merely an in-depth understanding on a chosen subject matter. It becomes a thorough understanding of the input/process/output system operating at every level—individual, organization, and the enterprise—and its constant shifts and changes in response to the global economy. (Figure 5.10.)

24. Knowledge in the System Approach is also the awareness of the input/process/output system description of the problem. Analysis of the problem, based on internal causal relations, external causal relations. As a final aspect, knowledge in the System Approach refers to the ability to synthesize where core competencies at every level are integrated to deliver quantum changes in the system output or to create novel solutions to the problem. (Figure 6.6.)

"Now, I turn to Mr. Scott Sealy, Human Resources Manager, to give his perspectives on the System Approach," concluded Mary Patterson.

"All these changes in the approach to problem-solving have been new to me," confessed Scott Sealy. "We have been too busy managing change in our company, from one wave to another. When Jack asked me to review Joe Whitehead's job description, I was very upset. It looked like Joe was all over the map, with no clearly defined boundaries for his organization.

His people were taking his leadership in this process of working across boundaries, seemingly causing concerns in other organizations. However, everyone appreciated the results. Joe and his team were helping everyone to be successful. When Jack asked for the review, I took the opportunity to review Joe's entire organization. I must admit, I am still confused. It appears that effective teams can form and dissipate, all on their own, when there is emphasis on solving the problem, rather than executing tasks. How does one recognize and reward these constantly changing dynamic teams, without clearly definable organizational boundaries? How do we reward someone like Mary who puts on all three hats—as a scientist, engineer, or manager—as needed in order to solve a problem?

"Perhaps one measure of performance recognition is how well the problem is defined and analyzed as an input/process/output system, and how new systems are synthesized. The second measure could be one of the scale or magnitude of the problem handled. This may be different from our current task-oriented organization, where the reward is based on the responsibility for budget, number of people, or other resources. Perhaps we can learn from the experiences of Mark Reardon in defining the new position for Linda Sanchez. We can learn from our own experiences, such as Joe Whitehead's new position of Product/Process Technology Manager.

"We are in a state of flux, but I am committed to the change process from task-oriented assignments to the system oriented solution driven responsibilities. My consolation is that I am not alone in this struggle. Linda Cook, our financial controller, has similar issues to deal with," Scott concluded.

Linda Cook began to speak with a tentativeness that reflected her state of mind. "All our financial processes and systems are based on tasks and how much we spend for these tasks. We call these activities that are clearly delineated as responsibilities among organizations. The organizational budgets are rolled up to achieve the enterprise budget. In recent times we have created project-based accounting, rather than activity-based accounting. From what I hear from everyone, in the System Approach each of us is working on projects all the time. The goal of every project is integrating resources from anywhere in the world, through our core competencies at every level—individual, organization, and the enterprise—to deliver highest value or benefit to the end-users around the world. (Figure 6.4.)

"I can see how this leads to entrepreneurial efforts with synergy among resources deployed. I can also see how redundancies within an enterprise, as well as between enterprises, can be reduced. This will require modification in our accounting practices far beyond what we are doing today," she concluded.

Jack Singer again took the floor. "This is our challenge, Linda. The challenge is to transition from task orientation to synthesis of solutions for large-scale improvements in the system output. We have done very well in our accounting and human resource functions to reduce costs by eliminating redundancies through the use of the tools of information automation. These are powerful tools for managing information. What we are managing in the accounting and human resources areas comes into focus when we get beyond tasks and activities. There are no clear solutions today. However, we must find them and soon," Jack concluded.

Finally, Congressman Ralph McCarthy spoke. "This meeting has been an excellent learning experience for me. Recently, I have held several town meetings with my constituents. In general, there is a great deal of apprehension about the future. Everyone is willing to help, but everyone is looking for direction. From this meeting I have learned that all of us have to make a collective transition. This is a change process for our society, from task-orientation to solving the problem as a whole. This implies learning to define the problem in terms of input/process/output systems, then applying the necessary core competencies at every level with an eye on achieving large-scale changes at the system output level.

"Traditionally, we are used to fostering and developing identified industries. First, it was mining, then steel making, automobiles, and then the service industries. Now we are into computers and software. Each wave of industrial advancement seems to be caught up in the challenges of the global marketplace faster than the earlier wave. As a nation, instead of relying on individual industries, we may need to rely on developing core competencies, and their simultaneous deployment at every level—individuals, organizations, and enterprises. This seems to be a tall order. Yet, individual instances I have come to witness during this meeting and elsewhere, truly provide me a glimmer of hope. After all, the concept is simple—the whole is greater than the sum of its parts. All along we have trained people to look at the parts in detail and assemble them into a unit. The time has come to look at the larger picture first and comprehend it fully, so that we can develop the details through selective synergy between core competencies.

"I have learned during this meeting that such an integral view of the problem could occur at an individual, organization, or enterprise level. Perhaps this transition is occurring more at the level of individuals than at the organizational level. This is not adequate unless all of us—individuals, organizations, and the enterprise—make a collective change from task execution to problem resolution orientation. The System Approach seems to provide a methodology for such a change process. While collective change at the enterprise level may be the most desirable outcome, I have learned that organizations and individuals should not postpone their transition from task execution to system oriented problem resolution. Change at the individual and organizational level may be both possible and necessary in anticipation of the enterprise level change. If the enterprise does not change, individuals and organizations can still survive and succeed in the global economy if they employ the System Approach.

"Global economy is integrally linked with various economic styles chosen by the nations of the world. We as a nation are fully committed to the concept of capitalistic economy. Yet, every global enterprise has to operate under a multitude of national economic styles. This may be perfectly acceptable as long as the enterprise is focused on all aspects of the system output, in other words, stakeholder benefits. (Figure 4.4.) Absent such simultaneous focus on all of the system outputs, any focus on individual system output, such as investor's benefits, may be deemed a continuation of task oriented enterprise management. It is the role of national leaders to foster approaches for system-oriented management, with a focus on quantum improvements in all of the system outputs. Such integrated vision may be a real and immediate need. Absence of such an integrated approach and vision may be reflected in the stagnant standard of living for a large cross-section of our population, even though the economy has been doing well for a long period of time. This shifting economy and its impact on individuals is noted as management's lack of value for their employees in the workplace.[24]

"If enterprises are likely to be global in their scope, then what role do state subsidies play in order to attract industries? Should we continue to focus on attracting individual industries, as we presently do, or should we attract industrial activities based on appropriate strength in core competencies? While the entire enterprise may not be located in a state, specific organizations of many enterprises could be attracted to a state based on core competencies. Thus, the states could focus on attracting specific organizations of the global enterprises. If the value added to the enterprise by these organizations is larger and better than anywhere else in the world, then employees in such organizations would enjoy the highest rewards, the highest standard of living in the world. In the future, the state subsidies may not be simply tasks or isolated initiatives for attracting manufacturing industries and jobs. Instead, they could be incentives to foster integrated development of core competencies at every level—individual, organization, and enterprise. This also sets a new paradigm for education and training at every level, from elementary schools to continuing education.

"All of these ideas and more set the stage for our vision of the next century. It is not simply a matter of doing more of the same, or even doing more of the same better. Our approach to the twenty-first century may have to be a vision of transition, from a collection of tasks and their execution to a vision of input/process/output systems at every level, and its deployment through a cluster of core competencies. While the opportunity seems endless, the change process appears to be daunting. Communication of this need for change in our society should be my single most important mission as we look ahead," concluded the Congressman.

• • •

Paul Gagnon could not wait to get home and talk to his wife. "Susan, it was an extraordinary meeting. There is a glimmer of hope in this struggle for survival in the global economy," yelled Paul as he entered the house.

"Honey, you must be talking about the System Approach. I have been trying to get your attention for so long. I am glad you are finally on the band wagon," replied Susan.

Appendix

Excerpts from the cover story titled "Economic Anxiety," in the March 11, 1996 issue of *BusinessWeek*.[1]

It's not just the unemployed, like Szilagyi, who are experiencing some cognitive dissonance these days. Real wages have been stagnant for most of the past two decades. The distribution of income among Americans has become more unequal over the same period. For most Americans, the workplace has become a far more capricious place. During the past decade, Corporate America has restructured, downsized, right-sized and reengineered millions of people out of their jobs, while putting the squeeze on the wages of remaining workers. At the same time, top executives promised that the payoff would come-first in higher productivity and then, labor is due, in higher wages.

Lost contract. *"People have a sense that these are*

changes radically different from anything they have seen before," says Claudia Goldin, an economic historian at Harvard University. Many workers lament the breakdown of the social contract between employees and employers—a contract that once made it possible to raise both a family and one's living standards. In a BusinessWeek/Harris Poll of 1,004 American adults, conducted in late February 1998, 77% of the respondents rated large corporations only fair or poor at providing job security for their workers, and 78% rated the companies similarly on their loyalty to employees.

The restructuring of Corporate America has carried enormous social costs. Nitin Nohria, a professor at the Harvard Business School, tracked the changes that engulfed 100 of America's largest companies—"symbolic markers of our well-being"—from 1978 to the present. He found that on a net basis 22% of the work force of these companies, or 3 million workers, were laid off during the period, and 77% of all layoffs involved white-collar workers.

Speak to workers, though they know that there's no turning back and that they are going to have to make some adjustments. "It's not like the old days when you graduated from high school and had the same job for 20 or 30 years," says Denis Velez, a 47-year-old commercial photographer. He had taken a job that pays $200 a week processing film at a Ritz camera shop in Deerfield Beach, FL, so he can get health benefits for his family. " Technology, especially in the field I'm in, is changing so much. In a couple of years, film itself will be obsolete."

Although workers realize they have to retool, many hope for guidance. So far, notes Shoshana Zuboff, a Harvard Business School professor and author of The Age of the Smart Machine, only a handful of companies have committed the resources to help their work forces develop new skills. Today, all corporations essentially have the same technology, the same networking systems, the same software, she says.

The only way they can beat out their competitors is by enabling their biggest asset, their work force, to be more innovative in using the technology to create new products and new services that sell well. Instead, throughout its decade-long restructuring, Corporate America has primarily viewed workers as liabilities rather than assets.

What about the payoff? Is Corporate America's wrenching transition creating an economy that can successfully compete in a global economy? Future economic growth is fueled by investment in physical and human capital. In both respects the U.S. is in far better shape than it was during the 1980s. Business spending on new equipment, financed by strong profits, has climbed to a record 8% of national output. In 1995, the manufacturing capacity of the nation's factories rose by 4.3%, the biggest increase in 25 years.

Not only do workers have newer and more sophisticated equipment on their jobs, but they also are becoming better educated. In 1987, 57% of high school graduates went to college soon after graduation. The percentage now is 62% and climbing, despite rising college costs. By comparison, the percentage of high school graduates enrolling in college hardly rose from the late 1960s to the mid-1980s. Among males the share going to college actually fell during the period.

Access to education is the key to success in a world where well-paid jobs for high-school graduates are vanishing and being replaced by managerial and professional positions. The challenge for America is ensuring that everyone has the chance to get the education and training needed to succeed. "The data is very clear about the relationship between education levels and economic success," says IBM Chairman Louis V. Gerstner Jr. "If our country can't get a sense of alarm and start educating the 30% to 40% at the low end, we are going to be in trouble."

"If America wants the benefits of expanding trade and technological innovation, it needs to do more to ease the

pain of transition. For corporations, that means better training programs, heightened sensitivity to the anguish of layoffs, and shared sacrifice by management."

"For policy makers, that means encouraging workers to gain new skills by introducing training vouchers and expanded investment retirement-type accounts to pay for tuition."

"Investing in human capital is not a new idea. It needs to be pursued aggressively, not merely be given lip service. If America doesn't respond to this challenge, the anti-business backlash already under way will worsen. The tenets that have made the American economy so competitive and vibrant will be in danger of being undermined."

Excerpts from the article, "How to Beat The Squeeze on The Middle Class," by Joseph S. Coyle, *Money Magazine*, May 1995.[9]

Job and income security. *In an increasingly competitive global economy, the certainty of employment is a thing of the past. In fact, a disturbing one out of six who responded to our "10th Americans and Their Money" poll reported that they or a member of their immediate family had been laid off in the past 12 months. And 64% of workers who answered the poll felt that if they lost their current job, it would be difficult to find a new one. That's a far cry from the job-for-a-lifetime America that made the middle class feel strong, if not rich, during the '50s, '60s and '70s. As for income security, in an exclusive interview with Money President Clinton summed up Americans' current state of mind: "It is the sense that even if there are more jobs, even if there is growth, even if there is low inflation, my income won't go up and my family situation won't be more stable."*

This article quotes several statistics. Here are a few.
- Household incomes are up, but only for families with two incomes,
- 37% of the middle class fear that their children will not

live as well as they do,
- 64% say it would be difficult to find a new job if they were fired.

The article continues:

Build up your tolerance for the shock of the new. "Jobs are going to be re-deployed, automated, eliminated and regenerated in forms we haven't yet imagined," writes Harry S. Dent Jr. in <u>Job Shock: Four New Principles Transforming Our Work and Business</u>. "The best way you can beat the pink slip is to broaden your skills and investigate all the different ways you can apply them in the job market," Dent says. What's more, Morris Schectman, author of <u>Working Without a Net</u> and a member of the Newt Gingrich brain trust, has this warning for any doubters: "Make sure your sense of security is portable or transferable; otherwise you're in big trouble." In short, you're on your own now: Make the best of it.'

References

1. Mandel, Michael J. "Economic Anxiety." *BusinessWeek* (March 11, 1996): 32-36.
2. Patterson, Rusty. "Knowledge Workers Sought." *Manufacturing Engineering* (June 1997): 108.
3. Marino, Sal. "Ultrapreneurs Work Smarter—Not Longer—Than Other Executives." *IndustryWeek* (July 7, 1997).
4. Council of Engineering Report. "Conclusions and Challenges." American Society of Mechanical Engineers (June 1997).
5. Sperry, Paul. "Are Economists Obsolete Today? New Economy, Old Thinking Threaten Profession." *Investor's Business Daily* (July 23, 1997).
6. Baker, Stephen. [Review of the book: The Future of Capitalism—How Today's Economic Forces Shape Tomorrow's World, by Lester C. Thurow]. *BusinessWeek* (March 11, 1996): 6.

7. Stein, Charles. "For Workers, It's The Age Of Anxiety—N.E. Study Recalls Nightmarish Spin On American Dream." *The Boston Globe* (January 21, 1996): 71 and 77.
8. Ackerman, Jerry. "What Price Good Jobs?—As Massachusetts Ponders Raytheon Aid, Other States Seek Way Out of Escalating Battle for Manufacturing Jobs." *The Boston Globe* (April 2, 1995): 75.
9. Coyle, Joseph S. "How to Beat the Squeeze on the Middle Class?—You Will Have to Work Longer, Harder and Smarter. But Follow Our Advice and You Can Move Ahead." *Money* (May 1995): 106–112.
10. Astley, Kevin R. "Title Needed to Combat Pseudo-Engineers" [Letter to the Editor]. *Mechanical Engineering* (August, 1997).
11. Warner, Joan et al. "Economic Anxiety—Clinging To The Safety Net; Most Nations Want To Streamline Their Economies Slowly." *BusinessWeek* (March 11, 1996): 40–41.
12. Hammonds, Keith H. et al. "Economic Anxiety—Writing a New Social Contract; O.K., Job Security is Dead. What Happens From Here?" *BusinessWeek* (March 11, 1996): 38-39.
13. Eds. "Managing Innovation—Know When Incremental Change Will No Longer Do." *Inside R&D* (January 18, 1995): 3-4.
14. Rose-Asch, Maralah S. "Finishing Business—Smaller is Replacing Bigger in Business." *Products Finishing*, (October 1997): 38-39.
15. Spielman, Joseph D. "Let Us Work Concurrently." *Manufacturing Engineering* (August 1997): 208.
16. Thomas, John B. "Down But Not Out." *World Traveler* (February 1996): 45.
17. Dietz, Dan. "Help Wanted: Engineers." *Mechanical Engineering* (August 1996): 46–50.
18. Eds. "In Our Pages: 100, 75 and 50 Years Ago: 1898—Economic Boom." *International Herald Tribune* (January 28, 1998).

19. Manning, William. "Surging Inequality and Falling Real Wages. How to Reverse the Trend?"[Review of the book *The American Corporation Today* by Lester C. Thurow]. *The MIT Report* (December/January 1997/1998): 7.
20. Prasad, Biren. "Use of Concurrent Engineering as an Integrator in the Product Development/Delivery Process." Proceedings of the Winter Annual Meeting of the American Society of Mechanical Engineers. (November 17-22 1996).
21. Drucker, Peter F. *The Effective Executive.* New York: HarperCollins Publishers, 1967.
22. Brelis, Mathew. "A Boom Beyond the Reach of Many" *The Boston Globe* (May 3, 1998): G1 and G2.
23. Eds. "Unit Manufacturing Processes—Issues and Opportunities in Research." Washington, D. C.: National Academy Press, 1994.
24. National Public Radio (Report by David Molpus). "Parental Pressures." Morning Edition, Washington, D. C.: National Public Radio (February 26, 1999).